The Diary of Captain William Buchanan

An Historical Novel of Canadian Pioneer Courage

by J. Frank Sexton

2nd Edition, July 2014

(This edition is also available as an e-book.)

Cover Design by J. F. Sexton

ISBN: 978-0-9878820-2-8

Dedication

This novel is dedicated to all those who sacrificed everything to build this country.

One of those was my great-great-great-great-grandfather, William Buchanan. He immigrated to Nova Scotia from Scotland in 1784 where he carved a homestead out of the wilderness with no one upon whom he could rely except a few kind neighbours. He then abandoned that home hoping to find something even better, trekking to the very edge of civilization in Upper Canada on the north-west shore of Lake Erie.

There he met and married a woman of Dutch descent from an United Empire Loyalist family and raised six children without the loss of a single child to disease or injury.

But war broke out in 1812 and he laid down his own life in defence of all that he had worked so hard to gain. The truly sad irony is that he never knew that due to his sacrifice, and the sacrifice of many others whose names have been lost over the years, the invasion was turned back and his descendants would prosper in a place that would eventually become Canada.

His sacrifice was not in vain. He gave everything without ever knowing what he helped to win; a true act of selflessness and heroism.

Acknowledgements

I spent more than a year researching the lives of both William and Elizabeth. Nearly all of that time was spent tracking down leads on the Internet using the major search engines and the genealogy site, "ancestry.ca". I also followed leads provided by individuals with whom I came into contact.

I would be remiss, however, if I failed to mention those libraries that are endeavouring to digitize many old books and manuscripts through imaging. While some of these documents are very difficult to read because of the outdated style of handwriting, blurred pages, stains, etc., when you find a hand-written ledger that is more than 200 years old containing the actual signature of your ancestor, the image literally pushes you back in your chair and you forget to breathe for just a moment. The image of my great-great-great-great-grandfather's signature in a paymaster's journal acknowledging the receipt of his pay, is literally the only personal thing that I have of his. Therefore, to all you anonymous librarians toiling to preserve these old documents, please know you have earned my eternal gratitude.

The Diary of Captain William Buchanan

Table of Contents

Part 4: Husband and Father (1800-1812)..................**101**

Part 1: The Discovery of the Diary

The Lucky Man

Happenstance is a strange thing. By its very nature, it can never be predicted and hoping for its blessing is a waste of time. And like the ticking of a clock, the millions of tiny happenings that make up a lifetime are mostly meaningless and forgettable.

And yet I have noticed both in the people around me and throughout history that some lives seem to attract a number of accidental events that propel them to great prominence or success. But I have also heard, and believe, that the lucky man works very hard for that luck.

Never having known my own grandparents who either died before I was born or died before I could form any memory of them, my ancestry was a great unknown. But for most of my life, it was an unknown that was of lesser importance than most of the other mysteries I worked hard to study and understand.

When I retired, however, I developed an interest in my family's history and started to dig. Digging into the past can be very difficult and I have spent endless hours following many leads most of which proved false. But whenever some bore fruit, it made the effort worth while.

It was during one of those dreary and tedious periods that happenstance became my friend. Travelling back to where much of my mother's family had lived for the past two hundred years, I saw on the Windsor evening news how a crew digging a foundation had found an old chest containing some documents and journals. The reporter talked about how they dated back to the War of 1812 and then mentioned a name. That name made me sit up with surprise. It was the name of one of my great-great-great-great grandfathers, William Buchanan.

I grabbed my laptop and quickly found the station's web site. Writing to them, I asked them to put me in contact with the person who found the chest since the contents appeared to originate from one of my ancestors. I thought that, at the very least, it might make a good human interest story for them.

The next day I got a call from the reporter who had prepared the original story. He told me that he had spoken to the man who had dug up the chest and would like to introduce us and do a follow-up. I could barely contain my excitement and explained that I was only in the area for a short time so hoped he could arrange something in the next day or so. The reporter said that first he had some questions for me and if it was convenient he could come by right after lunch. It was obvious that he wanted to do some background checking to ensure I was who I claimed to be. So I gave him the motel's name and address and my room number. I told him I would be here at one o'clock waiting for him.

A van with the station's markings pulled in right on time and I opened the door to greet him and his cameraman. We shook hands enthusiastically as he introduced his colleague carrying a bunch of equipment on a wheeled dolly. He explained that he'd like to interview me here before we left to gauge my expectations and get some background information on my ancestors before either of us knew what I would find in the chest. He was hoping to capture some additional angles to the story that way. I told him to set things up as he saw best and then we could get right down to it. He nodded to his assistant and then started the conversation.

He asked me if I had a copy of my family tree with me. I told him to have a seat while I got the files from my briefcase. Opening it, I pulled out two heavy binders and a folder and dropped them down on the little round table which seems to grace every motel in which I have ever stayed.

The reporter seemed very impressed by the sheer volume of paper and asked if he could make arrangements to copy the relevant pages to make sure he got all the names and dates correct. I told him that I would be glad to drop by his office for that purpose although I suggested it might be faster just to take pictures with his smart phone.

Then, in preparation for the interview, I showed him my family tree back to both William Buchanan, the son, and William Buchanan, the father, answering his questions as we went. Based on his original reporting, I said it sounded like the father was the author of the journal, but wouldn't know for sure until I examined it.

At just that point, his assistant started to switch on the lights which made me jump a little when the first one came on. Seeing that, the reporter asked if I had ever been in front of a camera and, when I said no, he gave me some helpful suggestions and we got rolling.

After about twenty minutes of me answering his questions, he thanked me, turned to the camera, gave what I suppose was a standard closing statement, told the cameraman to stop and we were done. Quizzing him about the length of time we had taken, he indicated that the piece would get edited down to fit the air-time the producers decided to give it.

One of the most difficult questions he had posed to me was about my expectations. I really couldn't spell them out in any great detail except to say that I was hoping to really learn about the kind of people my ancestors were, instead of just having a collection of dates and dry facts about them. I hoped that the contents of the chest would bring William and his family to life for me.

As the cameraman packed up his gear, the reporter asked if I would like a ride with them to the site. I told him that I wanted a chance to start reading the documents and wondered if that would take up too much of their time. He said not to worry but that if time did become an issue he would ask the fellow who dug up the chest to allow him to bring it back into town. So I said let's go and we were off.

The drive to the site near Leamington wasn't actually that far, but as everyone knows when you're anxious with expectation, even short trips can take an eternity. Nevertheless, we arrived in a little more than a half-hour and got out to meet the guy running the backhoe.

He was a big man but very friendly and led us over to the mobile trailer that was on the site. He kept asking me, with a wink, if I was sure my ancestors wouldn't have hidden some valuables in the chest to go with the documents. I kept assuring him that they were not rich but he was welcome to keep examining the chest "just in case".

Then, when we stepped into the trailer, I saw it sitting right before my eyes. The chest wasn't very large, maybe a foot wide by eight inches deep and six inches high and it was rather plain with just the iron straps holding it together. I saw right away where he had broken off the lock, which at first annoyed me because I would have preferred that he hadn't damaged it, but I held my tongue and quickly reminded myself that a broken lock just didn't really matter.

Suddenly, though, it really hit me. I was standing beside a piece of my own history. I couldn't help but feel a little shiver run down my spine as our host lifted the chest's lid.

I looked down at its contents for what seemed an eternity until the stillness was broken by his voice asking if I was going to lift the papers out and have a look or not. I jerked my head away from the chest, saw his smiling face and simply apologized for losing myself for a moment.

Truth be told, though, I was almost scared to touch them. I slipped my backpack off and got out the small magnifying lamp and cotton gloves I had bought in Windsor. The gloves were about the only precaution I could remember when handling old documents.

Then I sat myself down and gently, as if it all might fall to dust upon my touch, lifted out the leather-bound journal along with some pages that were tied on top of it with a piece of old twine. The leather was dry and in danger of cracking, but I took hold of one end of the twine and slowly and gently pulled on it to undo the bow. Thankfully, the twine slid apart with surprising ease and I lifted it and the pages away from the journal.

Glancing at the pages as I sat them down, I noticed that they were actually written by Elizabeth, William's wife, and dated shortly after his death. So I picked them up and started to read.

But I was quickly taken aback as her fear and anger exploded off the pages.

It was hard to put myself in her shoes since the United States is now such a close ally and good neighbour, but Elizabeth's reality was much different. Her family was of Dutch descent and had been loyal to the British crown during the American revolution. Her own great-great-great-great grandfather, Theunis Quick, was among the first 200 Dutch settlers in New Amsterdam, now Manhattan. In fact, the Quick home was directly across from the fort he helped to build on the southern tip of the island. Her roots were, therefore, very deep in the New World.

War had pushed her family to the very edge of civilization where they, no doubt, had thought themselves safe from the revolution. As loyalists, they were granted land on the north shore of Lake Erie in Upper Canada and had to start their lives again in this wilderness. The only real access to that part of Upper Canada was via ship on Lake Erie from the Niagara area. Road access was only made possible some twenty to thirty years after the war when Lord Talbot commissioned a route along the lake shore.

For her, less than thirty years after the Treaty of Paris in 1783 ended the American Revolution, it must have seemed that the war she and her family fled was still pursuing them with deadly intent. Indeed, the threat for her was very real.

Looking at the date of the note, she could not know that the British would successfully defend their colonies and even take the battle back to the Americans before the war ended a year later in 1814.

For me, reading her letter was more precious than finding a chest of gold. Believing that happenstance would not have brought me here for no good reason, I saw that her fear and anger were the emotions of a real person, not just some name with dates attached. In that moment, I made a silent resolution that I would do my best to publish the contents of these documents, not only for the sake of history, but also as a memorial to two ordinary human beings whose extra-ordinary struggles helped to make this country. In my head, I knew that it was a leap of faith to think that the journal would be as exciting to read as Elizabeth's letter, but I simply could not bring myself to believe otherwise .

So please allow me to share what this stoke of luck brought to me, the tragic but heroic story of William Buchanan, one of my great-great-great-great-grandfathers.

Part 2: Elizabeth's Note

Editor's Note:

This is Elizabeth's letter which she wrote and buried with William's journal. There was a perfect bow holding them together, expressing her grace and dignity even in her most desperate hour. While the letter speaks for itself, one cannot help but think that she was near panic when she wrote it, having been widowed only a few weeks earlier. She would have been thirty-three years old with six children to raise, the oldest being just eleven. Making things worse, her home, just north-west of Point Pelee, was now under American occupation. Her mother had passed away in 1807 at the age of fifty-five and, while her father was still alive, he would have been sixty-three in the fall of 1813 so she could not realistically look there for help. It must have seemed like the world was truly ending for her.

Still, the handwriting was impeccable even if the letters were written in a style that has long since ceased to be taught. It was almost flowery, and definitely elegant. Clearly, she took her time to draft the letter but kept it short and to the point. There were some stains on the old paper, one or two looking like they could have been made by her tears, but it was remarkably well preserved after being buried for 200 years.

As I transcribed both Elizabeth's and William's handwriting, I took the liberty of updating the more obscure words and grammatical style in which English was written two hundred years ago to make the text more understandable to the contemporary reader. Having said that, I also tried to keep as close as possible to the flavour of the language so that the reader might better empathize with their times.

The Letter

Monday, October 25, 1813

To whomever may find this,

My heart has been torn from my chest and now it is being trampled into dust by that which fate has deemed to be my destiny. I have yet to still the flow of tears that have stained my cheeks for the past month when my dearly beloved husband was taken to our Lord's side. But now further injury looms like a ghastly apparition in the darkest night.

The treasonous evil from which my family fled a mere thirty years ago has invaded this colony. It has shattered the tranquillity that we toiled in peace and happiness to hew out of the wilderness and brought with it the shadow of death and destruction. These Kentuckians, as they call themselves, have pursued the King's loyal soldiers deep into the Thames valley and I have been reliably informed that they have even slaughtered the valiant Chief Tecumseh. While his Indian warriors were frequently ill disciplined, something upon which my husband oft commented, they proved their loyalty to our King time after time. William also spoke with admiration of the dignity with which Chief Tecumseh conducted himself when he dined with the officers at the Fort. Thus, with the news of the Chief's death, my spirit has sunk to such a new depth that I fear it can never be redeemed.

But now, just when I thought that I could be injured no more, I have learnt that my husband's grave has been desecrated in the most heinous and despicable manner. The Americans, in their great haste to fortify their ill-gotten gains, have begun to raise new ramparts over the consecrated ground where my husband lays. His body, barely cold in the ground, has now become part of the foundation of the invader's new fort. And I fear that these new battlements will frustrate any attempt by our most brave troops to push the Americans out. Thus, with that terrible possibility in mind, I trust you will forgive me for praying that as my husband's body returns to the dust, as all of our corrupt bodies must, it may cause the fortress walls to collapse like those of Jericho at the sound of the trumpet.

Despite enduring such pains and trials, I must keep my wits about me. I have my six precious children to protect as well as the memory of my dear husband. Since I have no wish to aid the enemy, even by accident, it is with the utmost of sorrow that I commit his journal to the very soil he worked so hard to make fruitful. I have not had the courage to open its pages and thus reawaken its memories but I cannot risk its discovery because it may contain information of a military nature that could be of value to our enemy.

My husband and I toiled for the past thirteen years to create our own garden of plenty. It is a good place and he and I were blessed to have reaped its bounty and to have raised a family on it. The land is rich and fertile, with bountiful sunshine and nourishing rain in the summer. And thankfully the winters are not so brutal that they would confound our souls. Thus it is indeed fitting to bury my husband's journals here since this is the place that we treasured throughout our all-too-short time together.

If fate should reveal to you this history, I earnestly hope and pray that the times will have changed for the better and that the King's majesty once again renders this land peaceful and prosperous. I have not told a soul of my actions for fear a word may be spoken however innocently that may lead to its discovery. With its burial, I am putting aside a part of me that I must for the sake of my own future and that of my children. May God look kindly upon my actions and deliver us from this darkest of times.

Despite my despair, I remain,

A loyal and humble servant of his majesty,

(signed) Elizabeth Buchanan

Part 3: Adventurer (1787–1800)

Editor's Note

The Historical Context

News travelled slowly in the late eighteenth and early nineteenth centuries. It took about twelve weeks, or three months, for a ship to cross the Atlantic bringing with it the mail and all the latest news from the old world. It could take many more days or weeks to be delivered to the frontier settlers.

But this was a time of great change in Europe. Following the American Revolution, French society underwent a profound and violent shift. The Bastille was stormed in July of 1789. King Louis XVI was beheaded in 1793 as the reign of terror initiated by Robespierre took the lives of many of the aristocracy. The other royal houses in Europe were shaken and fearful of revolution taking hold in their lands.

As a result, England decided that her remaining colonies in North America needed to be defended to act as a bulwark against the American republican ideas and to show the upstart Americans that England remained a great world power. A program was begun in her remaining colonies to build fortifications and ships to defend the frontier. Even the governance of the colonies was revised by dividing what was previously known as "Quebec" into two parts, one recognizing the majority French culture in Lower Canada and the other recognizing the flood of Loyalist settlers north of the Great Lakes in Upper Canada. The other two colonies, Nova Scotia (which at that time included present day New Brunswick and Prince Edward Island) and Newfoundland (which included the north shore of the Gulf of St. Lawrence and the Labrador coastline) were similarly strengthened.

England sought out alliances with the aboriginal peoples who had been pushed west by the Americans, not because of any heart felt sympathy, but because they calculated the worth of such an alliance in a time of conflict. Tribes that fled the new United States were given land in either Upper or Lower Canada and even allowed to bring their slaves. Chief Brandt of the Six Nations personally owned some forty slaves which he brought with him from New York.

Slavery in the aboriginal communities was common and was the result of prisoners being taken during periods of war rather than being imported over the ocean. Their slaves sometimes even included colonial settlers who were often sold back to the their own communities in return for more durable goods.

While perfect harmony did not exist between the settlers and natives in the four remaining British colonies, there seemed to be a certain *modus vivendi* between the two communities based on their mutual distrust of, and animosity directed at, the Americans. There are few records of any major conflict between the tribes settled in Upper Canada compared to the constant raids and low level warfare in the Ohio Valley, Kentucky and Indiana.

Back in England, the industrial revolution was just starting to gain momentum and many indentured labourers on the great estates were being pushed off the land in favour of large-scale industrial farming. This helped to provide an incentive for many people to risk the voyage to the New World where they hoped to find new opportunities, opportunities that were just not possible in the rigid class structure of England and Scotland.

William's World

It was into this maelstrom of momentous upheaval that William sailed to Nova Scotia, leaving his native Scotland at the tender age of ten. Today we would be horrified at a child of ten embarking on his own across the vast ocean, but things were quite different then. Boys of twelve, thirteen and fourteen were fighting and dying on the front lines of armies. Children were often thought to be adults once they reached puberty and many married in their mid-teens. To be apprenticed out at the age of ten would have been a great opportunity for William and, despite any misgivings about leaving his native Scotland, he would have tried very hard to live up to the privilege that he was provided. He would never have been able to achieve the things he did had he remained an indentured farm labourer or fisherman in Scotland.

So he said goodbye to his native town of Kirkcudbright and the surrounding gentle rolling hills that guide the River Dee down to the

Irish Sea. Like many young men and women from that district, there was really nothing left for him in Scotland except fond memories.

William was not very dedicated to keeping his diary on a daily basis. It became clear early in my reading that he wrote when and if he had time or there were important things that he wished to commit to paper. While he was now, at least in his own mind, an adult and master of his own domain, I had to keep reminding myself of his real age and thus be satisfied with his infrequent entries.

He was mostly focused on the events that he and his neighbours were experiencing, although I was often surprised by his awareness of what was happening 3,000 miles across the ocean. He also expressed his contempt for the "democratic" experiment to the south in a number of entries throughout his diary.

But I could see the loneliness creeping into his life as he grew into real manhood. He could not find a companion while in Nova Scotia and so, when the opportunity arose, he jumped at the chance to try elsewhere to find happiness.

I doubt that he grasped the significance of moving from Nova Scotia to Essex County in Upper Canada, or felt that any great destiny awaited him. He simply wanted to establish a home and family of his own. He was clearly unskilled at relationships and I do not think he understood how his future father-in-law was probably anxious to have Elizabeth marry him and manoeuvred the two of them accordingly. Elizabeth's father, John Quick, had good reason to be anxious for his daughter since there were not many other settlers close by and fewer still that were eligible bachelors. Nevertheless, William's romantic instincts were sound as evidenced by his planting of a secret flower bed that, according to him, was foolishness because they could not be eaten or sold. It was wonderful to feel his happiness grow as the romance deepened.

I should mention that throughout the diary William refers to holidays which are no longer celebrated in Canada and expresses values in the old non-decimal English currency. Therefore, I have added explanatory footnotes as appropriate to help the reader. I have also created footnotes where I felt it necessary to explain any other entry that may not be obvious to the reader.

Sunday, April 8, 1787

It is Easter Sunday and I have much for which to thank God. But, as the good Reverend reminded us all this morning of the seven deadly sins and how Jesus took all our sins upon himself this day, I realized that I have committed the sin of sloth by not writing anything in my journal until now.

My father gave me this wonderful leather-bound book as a parting gift when I left Scotland some three years ago and since my arrival on these shores on August 21, 1784, I have not written a single entry. I do hope dear father will forgive my thoughtlessness regarding such a fine gift. At least, I can thank the school masters in Kirkcudbright for having the fortitude to teach me enough English to finally sit down with some confidence and begin documenting my adventures in this book.

Just looking at it brings back memories of father's stern warnings on the day we parted. "Obey the ship's officers!" he said. "And commit everything that you experience to memory so that one day you too might become a great sailor like Captain Cameron. And always remember that your future depends on the good graces and references that the Captain may or may not give you based on your behaviour and obedience. Learn from everything you see and hear. And most importantly, keep the wonder of God's great creation close to your heart for as long as you live."

It has been three years since I last saw him standing on the dock. I do not know if I shall ever see him, my mother or any of my brothers and sisters again. But I am not melancholy because it is in this new world that I am certain my fortune lies.

But now to the task more immediately at hand. Allow me to recount some of my adventures since bidding farewell to Scotland. I cannot offer a complete accounting of my time during the past three years since too much time has passed for my memory to retain every single detail, but there are a number of things about which I feel compelled to write. These events will forever have a place in my memories, although they are not all pleasant.

The voyage itself was a ghastly narrative on the true size of the ocean between Scotland and New Scotland, or Nova Scotia as the gentry would have us say. For nearly twelve weeks the captain steadfastly spurred us on despite the two storms we encountered. The other officers told me that they were but a trifle compared to some of the storms they had encountered sailing to Jamaica, but still they were most terrifying for me. One man was swept overboard by a huge wave and never seen again. I remember the Captain reading from the Holy Scriptures in memory of the lost man. It made me angry when I overheard several sailors comment on how the man was the agent of his own misfortune for not lashing a rope around his waist. How could they speak so ill of the dead!

As the weeks dragged on, the food that the cook prepared steadily declined in appeal. When I saw my first weevil making its way through my biscuit, I nearly choked. But those around me laughed, slapped my back and explained how I was lucky to get some fresh meat for dinner. I failed to see the humour, but as the prevalence of various insects in the food became unmistakable, I learnt to simply accept what was offered and be grateful. Hunger will out, as they say.

At least we, the crew, had provisions to keep us fed. Some of the people who had purchased passage were not so fortunate. They were aware that passage included only space for them and their goods and that they were required to provide their own food and drink.[1] But as the trip entered its final weeks some of them ran short and began to beg us and other passengers for assistance. Despite strict orders not to give away any of our provisions lest we ourselves ran short, I did take pity on one young woman and gave her some old bread one day. I will forever remember her smile that day and I hope she fared well after we landed.

The Captain was always kind to me, perhaps because I was apprenticed to him for the voyage and I made every effort to meet his requirements. But I did witness how stormy his countenance could become when faced with any malcontent among the crew. Despite his fierce demeanour, I only witnessed general punishment administered once but I would not wish to witness such a thing again. The man was given ten lashes for falling asleep on watch, a punishment which could have been much greater had this man not been such an exemplary seamen throughout the voyage. Still, the whip tore his flesh and there was much blood. I felt just for a moment that I might collapse in a faint but rallied my strength so as not to embarrass myself.

Two persons, an unrelated man and woman, who had booked passage on the ship lost their lives to a fever, but the ship's doctor kept them well away from everyone else to the great relief of all, so their infirmity did not spread throughout the ship. It was sad to see the grieving children of the woman who succumbed, but at least they still had their father.

When we finally arrived at the great harbour of Halifax, I was overjoyed to see land again. My legs were unsteady as I stepped onto the shore. But I did not stay long in that settlement because it did not seem there were many good prospects for a young Scot like myself there. So I joined a group of settlers who were given land in Queen's County to the south-west of Halifax.

Land! My own land! I just celebrated my thirteenth birthday last January and I am already a landowner. I know that father would be so proud of me. I wish both he and mother could visit and see what I have already accomplished. Back home, the Earl owned all the land and the rest of us merely worked it for him to earn a small share of the profits to keep us alive. Even though there are great trees to be cleared and a house to be built, it is mine. I really must write to father and tell him every detail. I just know how proud he will be.

Sunday, May 6, 1787

I cannot believe that an entire month has gone by since I last wrote in this journal with barely a notice. Two of my neighbours, Allan MacPherson and John Fraser, have helped me finish my cabin. All of the folks around Port Mutton Harbour have been exceedingly kind to me and I have tried to repay that kindness as best I can. While I am not very skilled at some of the necessary tasks, at least my sinews can be put to good use and I can watch how the others do those things.

My cabin is a humble place, having only one room, but it has a good hearth with a sturdy chimney and it will do very nicely. I will need to make some furniture so it will be more like a home but that will come in time when the weather is unfit to work outside.

Last Tuesday was Beltane[2] and a group of us lit a hearty bonfire in celebration. This is a good place and I am content.

Tuesday, August 29, 1787

I am writing this entry because of events south of us. In that new country, called The United States of America, their parliament, which is called by another name of which I am not certain, has passed an act to permit settlement in their north-west territories. It appears to those of us who have put thought to such things that these rebels are trying to spread their form of unnatural government as far as possible with no regard to the wishes of others. I speak of both the French who pushed far into this vast continent more than 150 years ago and the English who explored the north and established a great company to profit from the enormous natural wealth of this land. Even the Indians must feel threatened by this new law.

American settlers now will be able to claim land to the south of Lake Erie, west of Lake Huron and south of Lake Superior, and thus hinder the growth of our own numbers from the Quebec Territory. One would have thought after the Treaty of Paris just a scant four years ago, that those rebels would have been content with their gains, but they seem a people emboldened by their military victory over our Sovereign King to press for even more.

Thursday, September 20, 1787

A man came around on horse back and told me that he was taking a census of all residents of Queen's County and that I was obliged to answer his questions. For all his high and mighty attitude, it did not seem to be an inconvenience so I told him that I would be happy to oblige him.

However, I was soon to feel embarrassed not by his questions but by the looks I received when I told him that I was the only resident here. He looked over his spectacles and said, "You have no wife or dependents?"

From his tone and looks, I thought that I had done something wrong by not being married or having a family so I repeated in a meek voice that I was indeed the only person living here.

He leaned over his papers and scribbled something. "So that makes you the head of the household, correct?"

I thought for a moment that his logic was so elementary as to be stupid but I held my tongue. I learnt on board ship never to question an officer or, in this case, an official. So I replied, "Yes Sir, I am the head of this household."

He smiled and asked a few more questions before thanking me for my co-operation. Then he simply packed up his papers, said goodbye in a very perfunctory manner, got on his horse, and trotted off.

I suppose the King needs to know how many of us live here, but I do wish he could have found a more pleasant man to visit. It is rare thing to have company and I had high hopes of hearing good news from a cheerful source to brighten my day. But it was not to be.

Many things have happened over the summer and I have been so occupied that I have not had time to add to this journal.

All of us who moved here help each other to clear the land. We also share our skills and animals to make the land fruitful. I have had a good summer, growing enough to last the winter and even to sell some, the money from which has allowed me to put aside a small amount for the future. I have dried and smoked a number of fish and salted the meat from some small creatures that I have trapped so I should have a good supply of meat through the cold that is to come. Winter is not that much colder than I remember in Scotland but during the last winter there was more snow than I could ever have imagined. I have heard that further inland to the north of the Bay of Fundy it can be much colder and I am glad not to live there.

Wednesday, October 31, 1787

It is the eve of All-Saints Day[3] and I sit in my own cabin surrounded by the most magnificent colours of nature in the trees. I give thanks to the Almighty for my neighbours who helped build this home to shelter me against the coming winter.

Starting this past spring, it was an enormous feat to fell the trees and then to draw out the massive roots with a great winch to clear a suitable bit of land to be sown. But at least those trees will provide sufficient warmth as they burn in my hearth through the winter.

But what a difference this new land brings. At home it is Samhain and many poor unfortunate servants will be given their leave and left with no way to support themselves. Here, such a tradition is not acknowledged since there are no servants in great houses to be sacked. I rather like this new land.

Tuesday, December 25, 1787

It is Christmas Day again and I sit here alone thinking of my parents. It will be their eighteenth wedding anniversary on Friday. How I wish I could be there to wish them well on that day. I can only hope that they know my prayers are with them for many more years of happiness.

Friday, March 21, 1788

It is the first day of spring and all afternoon the sun was shining brightly over the remaining snow. I trust that the last remnants of winter will soon melt and become a distant memory as the days get longer and warmer.

It is also Good Friday and I pray that the coming season will be as bountiful as the last one was. I will try to clear another few acres and so be able to plant a little more than last year and, with good Providence on my side, put away a bit more money.

I have not yet imagined what I shall do with my profits, but father always cautioned me not to spend coins that I did not yet have in my possession. So I shall just work as hard as I can and decide later what to do with any bounty with which I might be blessed.

Friday, August 1, 1788

It is Lammas Day[4] and the new wheat has grown well. The hay is thick and ready to be cut and baled. I am well satisfied with how well this growing season has progressed. I should make a handsome return this year.

Thursday, January 1, 1789

It is New Year's Day and I sit here in my warm cabin thinking of family thousands of miles away. Christmas was less bleak this year because I was invited to the home of John Fraser who has given me more assistance in the past two years than any man deserves. His wife, Mary, cooked an enormous goose and we all ate until we could eat no more. I owe them both a huge debt of thanks.

At least this winter has not been so bleak or seen as much snow as before. I hope that the coming months remain as mild.

Sunday, April 12, 1789

It is Easter Sunday and all day the sun brightened the spring sky. It was a truly beautiful day and I went outside to think about where I should clear more land.

To the north-west, there is a small natural meadow not far from the land that is already cleared. I think I shall expand in that direction to take advantage of what nature has provided.

I have invested in a good plough which I shall share with my neighbours. It means that there will be several ploughs between us and we can get the spring ground turned that much faster. Plus it is a means by which I can contribute to the common good from which I have benefited for too long without returning something.

Monday, September 21, 1789

It is the first day of autumn and I have been so busy this summer that I have once again failed to record anything in this journal. If I had not been so productive, I would truly be ashamed of my laziness.

Thanks be to the Lord, I have been fortunate to reap a good harvest and made a considerable profit because of the misfortunes of some of my neighbours. A blight infected a number of their fields but mercifully my own fields were spared. Although I feel somewhat guilty having profited from their misfortunes, the price I received was much better than I had expected.

I remember father receiving 1/- a bushel for oats and half that, or 6d, for a bushel of barley. But I got the enormous sum of 2/3 for my wheat.[5] I am almost embarrassed at the amount. I will put aside the money for the future.

Saturday, October 24, 1789

News has arrived that there has been an uprising in Paris. The central prison was attacked by a mob in July and there were many casualties on both sides. One has to wonder if this signals the beginning of the spread of American republicanism. I pray that this upheaval does not grow or spread any further.

It is, in point of fact, a wonder to me how ordinary folk could be so aroused as to rebel against their betters. I could understand if they had been occupied by some foreign prince, but this riotous behaviour in Paris is against their very own nobility. Even back home in Scotland we have become reconciled to the presence of the English and I do not think that the Scots would ever again mount a rebellion against the English monarchy.[6]

Thursday, January 14, 1790

It is my sixteenth birthday and I wonder about my future. I am still a bachelor and it seems a wee bit odd. But there are very few women of eligible age that live within reasonable distance such that I could get to know them. Still, I think I should be looking. Perhaps I should make discrete enquiries of the Reverend. Surely, he would understand my position.

Monday, May 10, 1790

I have decided to plant a few fruit trees at the north edge of my land. Back home in Kirkcudbright, father has written how the Earl has invested some great effort into orchards and greenhouses. One must presume that what is good for his Lordship might also be good here. So long as the trees are sheltered from the sea spray in harsh weather, I see no reason they should not do well. And I will not have to expend the effort that is now required to till the land. I hope it will be as simple as waiting for the fruit to ripen then pick it and take it to market.

Sunday, August 15, 1790

All but one of my apple trees have done well over the summer. I do not expect to have any apples this year to sell, but I can now plan to have an additional crop perhaps as soon as the year after next. Surely, I will have a good crop in five years as the trees mature.

I wonder about establishing a press instead of selling the fruit. A press would enable me to sell cider to the good folks here and maybe even in Halifax.

I must think about the cost and whether I can manage such a thing myself.

Friday, January 14, 1791

It is my birthday, but I must admit to feeling dreadfully melancholy. Another year has passed and I have been able to put more money aside, but I am so lonely. The winter cold and isolation is probably as much to blame as the lack of a companion.

I sometimes wonder if I have made the right decision to settle here. Is there something better elsewhere in this new land.

Monday, March 21, 1791

It is spring and my spirits have been lifted by the miracle of a beautiful warm sun rising in the east and brilliant crimson skies during the evening.

Easter is still a full month away on April 24. But I feel somewhat reborn now and saved from my awful black thoughts the past few months.

The land here is good and I will persevere.

Wednesday, September 21, 1791

The summer has been so busy and so productive. But I sense that same foreboding that I felt last winter. I must fight it off since I fear it will cause some ill humour to lay me low and there are no physicians nearby.

I must remain firm in the belief that I can do even better in the year to come and that I will find someone with whom I can share my good fortune.

Monday, January 16, 1792

News arrived today about a Royal Proclamation dividing Quebec into two separate entities, Upper and Lower Canada. I understand it was proclaimed on December 26 but news travels slowly.

I am not sure if this will have any affect on me but it is interesting to see that Lower Canada will retain its traditional French legal system while Upper Canada will be more like Nova Scotia with its British traditions.

It is said that this is to reflect the wave of Loyalists settling around Lake Ontario and Lake Erie. The old French traders gave names to much of the land and rivers, and even established a few villages, but many of these names are being slowly replaced by English ones since it is English folk who now inhabit the area.

I wonder if many Scots have moved to the new Upper Canada? It is said that the weather there is wonderful, bright, sunny and warm (even hot) in the summer but rather cold in the winter. I still remember the cold winds blowing off the Irish Sea as a child. Surely Upper Canada cannot suffer from the same bitter sea breezes since it is on much smaller lakes.

Thursday, November 29, 1792

It is unimaginable! The French mob has arrested their king, Louis. Apparently this happened last August. The mob has declared that France is no longer to be ruled by the monarchy but by a republic which I suppose will be modelled after the Americans.

I feel a sense of foreboding. First the colonies to the south of us declared themselves no longer to be bound to the King, now the French mob has done the same in France.

Will this bring war between the old and the new ideas? I hope that father and mother do not get involved in this foolishness.

Monday, April 29, 1793

Unbelievable! The post brought news that last January the French publicly executed their King. I remember from history that the English also took the head of one of their kings, Charles I, but that was more than a hundred years ago. Surely we have become more civilized since then. What is to become of France? I wonder what the French in Quebec are thinking today?

Saturday, May 4, 1793

More unbelievable news from the old country. France has declared war on England. Was it not enough that they chopped off the head of their king?

At least we know that the American President, George Washington, has declared that his country will remain neutral in all this mess which is a great relief to me.[7]

Friday, August 23, 1793

The news today is that Upper Canada has passed an act that forbids the importation of any new slaves. It came into force last July. That is at least a move in the right direction. I cannot believe that slavery is good for our souls. An honest man does his own work without complaint.

I wonder what is to become of the Negroes that are already in bondage. I have heard it said that the Indians also make slaves of those they capture in battle. Surely neither practice ought to continue in this modern world.

Wednesday, January 1, 1794

It is the beginning of another year. I have done well almost every year since I arrived in Halifax nearly ten years ago. I have even managed to save a considerable sum which I keep well hidden from any envious eyes. Perhaps I have saved so much because I have no family to support, but that is not a reason of which I can be proud.

My thoughts have wandered to the west and the possibilities there. But I do not know how such thoughts might ever come to fruition.

Thursday, July 10, 1794

The Americans have shown their contempt for the French efforts to recruit an army of American citizens to invade our land in support of their European war on England. In fact, the Americans completely abandoned their old revolutionary allies by passing a law last June making it illegal for the French to act in such a provocative manner on American soil.

Finally, some common sense has taken hold amidst the anarchy of republicanism.

Sunday, September 21, 1794

It is the beginning of autumn again and nature has been modestly good this year. I say modestly because the harvest was not as good as in the past. The rain was sparse and the weather cooler than normal. It makes me think again of the possibilities west of here.

I feel restless but perhaps that is just the boredom of ten years doing essentially the same thing.

Wednesday, January 14, 1795

I am now twenty-one years old but I feel much older. Despite my many good neighbours, I feel alone and empty. I suppose the snow and cold do not help my melancholy state but surely there is more to life than what I have experienced to date.

Friday, May 1, 1795

I do not think I will clear any more land this year. I have done enough and I do not think that I can properly manage any more since I know that I would feel obligated to sow and harvest any new space. It is as if I have reached a limit that my soul cannot breach.

Thursday, October 1, 1795

The good Lord has seen my ill-humour and, in His wisdom, has opened a path out of my malaise.

A neighbour has made an offer to purchase my land and I think I shall accept it. There are new opportunities deeper in the continent where there is rich land to be cultivated. I can take the money that I have saved along with the money from the sale of my land and begin again with much more land that I could ever have dreamt possible.

I am already twenty-one and have no family which is frustrating but if I can do well in the west then I can offer a potential wife a good home and life.

My mind races with the possibilities. Surely I will want to be close to the water so that I can sell my produce to a broader number of buyers. That means somewhere close to one of the enormous lakes in the west. I will have to travel to Halifax to learn more before I decide.

Thursday, December 10, 1795

I met with an agent in Halifax and, without much hesitation or deliberation, completed the arrangements to move west in the spring.

I will first sail to Montreal then go overland by wagon to Kingston. From there, I will board another ship that will take me to Newark via York. Then at Newark, I will have to take another wagon to Fort Erie where I will board a final ship for Amherstburg. The trip will take several weeks to complete.

The agent will take care of all the details, including the purchase of land in the Western District[8] where I hope to settle, letters of introduction to the other agents along the way and a letter to his contact in the district to welcome me on my arrival and guide me to my new home.

I hope I have done the right thing.

Saturday, March 26, 1796

My possessions have been loaded on board ship and I am happy to say that we are underway out of Halifax harbour bound for Montreal. It will be at least a couple of weeks before we arrive depending on the weather and how favourably the wind blows.

Wednesday, April 13, 1796

I stood on deck today watching the coast slide by as the ship sailed gently up the mighty St. Lawrence River. Although I have never seen it, surely the St. Lawrence must rival the great Thames River in England in both width and strength of current.

We passed Quebec City yesterday and will land at Montreal in another couple of days. The city of Quebec sits upon a great cliff overlooking the river and I cannot help but marvel at the achievement of General Wolfe taking the city thirty years ago.[9] It was sad that he perished just when victory was his.

Friday, April 15, 1796

We arrived at Montreal around noon and my crates were unloaded by early evening. I watched as they were hoisted out of the hold and set down on the dock. It took me somewhat aback that I had so little in this world and for a brief moment I wondered just what was I doing.

I paid a boy a full shilling to run to the agent here in Montreal who was to pick up my belongings and, good boy that he was, the agent appeared within about an hour. His assistants loaded up my goods on a wagon and I accompanied them to his place of business where I am now to stay the night.

Tomorrow, the true adventure begins with the trek to Kingston.

Tuesday, April 19, 1796

What a gruelling few days! First, in order to leave the Island of Montreal, we had to load everything on a barge that carried us across a substantial body of water which I was told was the junction of the Ottawa and St. Lawrence Rivers. To me, it was more of a lake than two rivers!

Arriving safely on the other side, we disembarked and set out across some very rugged trails stopping only to eat and setup camp for the night. This is rocky country lacking any good soil that I could see and it seemed to get even worse as we got closer to Kingston. I can only hope that the description of the Western District of Upper Canada does not disguise such unfavourable land in that part of the colony.

Although it is April, we passed some places that still had snow and ice on the ground, but that did not seem to impede our progress.

In any case, I am now safely in Kingston with my worldly goods and must await the schooner that will take me to Newark.[10]

Sunday, April 24, 1796

The schooner, Mohawk, arrived at Kingston harbour early this morning. She is a fine looking ship. I have heard that she was completed last May so is less than a year old. Of course, all of the ships on the Great Lakes have been built here in Upper Canada since none can sail past the rapids between here and Montreal. I am pleasantly surprised that, despite the colonial source of labour and materials, I can see no fault in her construction.

Because it is Sunday, the ship will be unloading its cargo tomorrow and then promptly loading up again to set sail on Tuesday for Newark via York.

Tuesday, April 26, 1796

I almost lost my crates when a stupid young man lost his grip on the ropes hoisting my possessions on board the ship. I wanted to thrash him severely, and would have done so if my possessions had fallen into the harbour.

Thankfully, the quick hands of another seamen saved the day and I am grateful.

Not having to wait for the tide, something that I shall have to get used to, we got underway shortly after all the holds were secured. As we sailed towards our destination, an incredibly lovely sunset coloured the sky in front of us and a light wind pushed us along at a good clip.

We should be at York[11] in a few days.

Saturday, April 30, 1796

With favourable winds, we made York early in the day. It has truly been blessed with a magnificent natural harbour.

I disembarked to stroll through the town but returned to the ship to eat and rest.

I found York to be a bustling small town and there are a great many merchants who have established themselves here. But I fear I shall not be a frequent visitor to this community and perhaps will not see it again.

Tomorrow morning, we set sail for Newark which is south-south-west of York on the southern shore of the lake.

Sunday, May 1, 1796

With a very brisk wind behind us, we made the crossing just as the sun was setting. But because it is Sunday again, the holds will not be unloaded until tomorrow.

I tried to seek out the man who would be taking me and my belongings to Fort Erie but to no avail. I was hoping to convince him to pass close to the remarkable waterfall that makes this part of the country so famous. But because I do not know their exact location relative to our route, I do not know if it will take extra time or if he will be willing. I suppose my request will have to wait until tomorrow.

It is funny how such a thing as wanting to catch a glimpse of this natural wonder can make a person so excited at the mere possibility. It makes me feel a little like a boy again.

Monday, May 2, 1796

The driver smiled when I asked about detouring to see the falls because, as he put it, it was really on the way and would not be a bother.

So I will see the falls probably tomorrow. There is simply no excuse for how giddy I feel. Thank goodness, none of my family or friends can see me behaving in such a childishly foolish manner.

Despite my mind being diverted, I overheard more than a few local people talking about the possibility of the capital of Upper Canada moving from here to York to be further away from the American border. Are we really that fearful of the Americans?

Tuesday, May 3, 1796

We arrived at the great falls of Niagara late in the day after climbing a seemingly endless cliff.

That cliff is the elevation over which the water tumbles and as we drew closer, I was struck dumb by the roar of the falls from even a great distance. But when I actually saw them, the enormous volume of water flowing over the falls is almost without measure and I stood amazed. A mist gently lifted itself from the churning river below and as the sun got lower, a rainbow appeared.

I am absolutely sure that this is a good omen as I start the last leg of my journey.

If I am fortunate enough to have a family, I must bring them here to see this for themselves. Mere description cannot do it justice.

Wednesday, May 4, 1796

We have reached Fort Erie on Lake Erie and none too soon. The ship on which I had passage booked was already docked and awaiting my arrival. I thanked the Captain profusely and explained that it was not my driver's fault but mine for wanting to stop and glimpse the falls. He smiled with a sort of knowing face and said we should get a move on and load my crates. He wants to be off tomorrow morning.

Thursday, May 5, 1796

We have left Fort Erie and are proceeding west on a beautiful bright sunny day with a brisk favourable breeze helping the ship. I love to stand on the fo'c'sle with my face leaning forward. It is so peaceful with only the sound of the wind filling the canvas and the water breaking on the bow. The horrible Atlantic almost made me forget the feeling.

I am also experiencing an unexpected elation and cannot wait to see Amherstburg. Will it be everything I hope? Only good Providence knows.

Sunday, May 8, 1796

Around mid-day today, when the ship started to turn to the north toward the mouth of the Detroit River, I went again to the fo'c'sle and strained my eyes for a first glimpse of Amherstburg. Then, like magic, I saw it.

Much to my disappointment, the first thing I saw was the fort built to protect it. It is sad that such a structure is needed for the protection of this wonderful settlement but the Americans still cannot be considered friendly.

But then I saw other buildings, people, wagons, horses, barrels and a number of other goodly sized ships in the harbour. Amherstburg is an unexpected piece of civilization in a place that I feared would have none.

When we docked, I disembarked quickly hoping to meet the gentleman to whom my agent had written last winter. But to my dismay, there was no one to be found because the ship was not expected until tomorrow.

So I shall put the wait to good use, put this pen down and take a walk through the town, stopping in at the tavern I spotted earlier. A wee dram to celebrate my arrival cannot be amiss!

Monday, May 9, 1796

The person to whom my agent wrote, Mr. John Quick, tapped on the door to my room quite early this morning and when I answered with a bit of mist in my eyes, he seemed to cast a certain look of disapproval on me.

But after I washed up and got dressed, we engaged in a very pleasant conversation as his wagon was loaded with my crates.

It seems that Mr. Quick's father brought the entire family from the United States when the British lost the war. Like me, neither of us understands how constantly changing rulers every few years can be good for a country. It is almost like a never-ending civil war with a new man coming to power bringing new ideas on how society should function but not ever having enough time to establish his vision before yet another new man replaces him and changes everything again.

It is remarkable how he and I see eye to eye on a great many things. I like this man.

Tonight, we camped some miles east of Amherstburg along side an old Indian trail that runs right to the Quick homestead which, I understand, is near my own future home. I asked about the danger from the Indians and he assured me in the most calming way that we had nothing to fear.

Wednesday, May 11, 1796

We arrived around mid-morning at the Quick homestead. John introduced me to his very charming wife, Elizabeth, and their numerous children.

I cannot but envy John and Elizabeth, but envy is a sin and I must push it away replacing it with a determination to attend to the issue rather than bemoaning it.

Tomorrow, John will take me and my belongings to the land that has been set aside for me. I know that I must clear a path along the front of the property to provide for horse and wagon travel and clear at least five acres in the first two years lest I be deemed forfeit of that land. Having done as much in Nova Scotia, this should not be too great a task.

Thursday, May 12, 1796

I am writing this from my new home! Well, let me quickly say that my home is, for now, a small shelter under which I can sleep.

During the past few days, the afternoons have been glorious and warm. At night, though, the temperature has been brisk but not cold. I can put up with that.

John has warned me, though, that when summer comes, the weather can become oppressively hot and humid, leading to great storms which darken the skies, bringing lightning and hail. It sounded so ominous that I think he was having some fun with me. Nevertheless, I humoured him. I know that time and experience will be my best teacher.

I have seen that many of the trees here are hardwoods, namely oak, walnut, hickory and maple, so perhaps I should not have been so confident about clearing the forest. But I am sure that my new neighbours will help, just as I received help when I first settled in Nova Scotia ten years ago. I have a great faith in the people I have met here to date.

I have but one complaint this lovely spring evening. I have been bitten by mosquitoes on virtually every inch of my skin. No sooner do I swat one than another takes a huge bite from me. Smoke from the fire seems to keep them somewhat at bay, but my eyes are not very fond of it. I have even begun to dread the next call of nature since these infernal beasts have no respect for a man's privy parts.

Wednesday, May 25, 1796

In less than two weeks, neighbours from all around have helped me to fell quite a number of trees and winched out their stumps. I have started little smouldering fires in the really deep rooted ones but I will have to watch them carefully lest those fires flare up and consume me as well!

The straightest and most suitable logs have been set aside and I will begin dressing them for my new home perhaps tomorrow evening.

But the land has given me its first big surprise! Ordinarily, I would use the stones unearthed by my plough to build my chimney and hearth, but this land is so rich that there are very few to be found! John and others have told me that a little to the east is a ridge made of gravel and stone where I can gather up what I require.

I really must refrain for complaining that the soil is too rich. But it is just such a surprise.

Saturday, July 9, 1796

Although I have been making progress on my cabin, having dressed most of the logs that will be needed, I was surprised today when a whole group of neighbours arrived with tools and food to finish the job. John Quick and Philip Fox each brought their two eldest boys and they were accompanied by the Brush brothers.

A couple of the men took their adzes and began to dress the remaining logs. Others started to dig out the trench into which the first logs would be placed.

Before I knew it, they had finished placing enough logs to reach my waist. Then they paused and asked where I'd like the door, hearth and some windows, so I put down markers for the door and windows and then the fireplace. With their big cross-cut saw, two of the men cut down through the logs for the door and then nailed a brace against them for the door frame.

To my utter amazement and heartfelt thanks, by the time the sun started to go down, they had everything done but the roof. However, darkness prevented them from making any further progress, so they laid down their tools and promised to come back tomorrow after church. Then they were off back home.

I am truly blessed with the most wonderful of neighbours.

Monday, August 1, 1796

I cannot believe that it is Lammas Day already and I have not put pen to paper for the past many weeks.

Lest anyone believe that I have been lazy, that is not the case. Not only is my humble cabin finished, but I managed to plant a few vegetables and some hay both of which are growing very nicely in this hot humid climate.

I am told that the heat and humidity that seems to settle in for days is the best kind of weather to grow corn. But I am not that familiar with the crop so I shall have to accept their word.

I have also gone out hunting with John and two of his boys, Joseph and David. We all had some luck and so I do not fear starving this winter as some have done. I also still have money from the old farm so, if need be, I can purchase supplies in Amherstburg this fall to tide me until Spring.

Friday, November 11, 1796

I was surprised to learn that the Dutch celebrate Martinmas[12] just as we Scots do. But more surprising was being invited to eat with the Quick family today.

All of the Quick women are wonderful in the kitchen. They fly through their tasks like a well-disciplined army and the result is as heavenly as one could imagine.

I noticed, after some time, John's eldest daughter who is named Elizabeth after her mother. Actually, I am ashamed to admit that I called out the name "Elizabeth" several times more than was really required since it always made both look my way. I really must curtail such behaviour before it is noticed.

Saturday, January 7, 1797

John Adams, the previous Vice-President of the United States, has won the election to become the second President of his country. He will assume his new office sometime in the next month or so. I have no knowledge of his leanings. Does he support France or will he follow Washington's example and steer clear of such nonsense?

Sunday, July 2, 1797

I went to the twenty-fifth wedding anniversary party for John and his wife, Elizabeth. They just had their seventh child, Elijah, this spring and she looks none the worse for it, thankfully.

I must say, their older children put on quite a feast! I probably should not write this down, lest it be read by the wrong eyes, but I found their eldest daughter, Elizabeth, to be blossoming in a quite attractive manner and her handling of the meal was magnificent.

In fact, although the party was in honour of the parents, I found that I could not, and still cannot, keep my mind off their daughter. I have searched my soul to discover if there is any evilness in this growing obsession, but she is so sweet and, above all, capable.

It brings a smile inside my head each and every time I think of her and how she dressed and moved.

I did not see any other men spend significant time with her, so dare I assume that she is not contracted to anyone yet? I must find out, discreetly of course. She will be fifteen this summer and John will, no doubt, be looking for a suitable match for her within the next year or so.

Monday, July 24, 1797

Having asked John's permission, I dropped off several bits of lace as a gift to Elizabeth on her fifteenth birthday. It was a mere trifle as they had only gathered dust in my trunk since arriving in Nova Scotia and I had no use for them. But Elizabeth was excited and spoke about how she could sew the pieces into the new dress she is making and how beautiful it will make it.

I know that I blushed at such attention and that others noticed my colour, but no one as much as cast a disparaging eye in my direction. There is hope, I think, that Elizabeth and I will come to know each other much better.

Thursday, September 21, 1797

It is the first day of autumn and my new crops have done well. Not only will I be able to sell some, but the money should permit me to stand on my own this winter without the gracious assistance of my neighbours.

I have heard from another neighbour, Mr. Adam Fox, that young Elizabeth has been talking about me with growing frequency. He thinks that I should approach John and ask him if I could come by to visit Elizabeth more frequently. I suppose that is the right and proper thing to do if I want this relationship to grow further.

Adam is a member of a large family that also fled the new republic to the south. Their family has roots in the state of Hesse which is part of the Holy Roman Empire. He explained that his family was conscripted by the local Elector (some sort of nobleman, I gather) and sent to America to fight for the British. I was ashamed that I had to ask where the state of Hesse was located. Adam smiled and told me if I would show him where Scotland is, then he would return the favour and show me where Hesse is. He has such a wonderful sense of humour.

Monday, December 25, 1797

I attended Christmas dinner at the Quick home earlier today. As usual, it was a marvel to behold and consume.

But I was, after some time, made the fool when I repeatedly thanked Elizabeth, John's wife, for such incredible food. Finally, she glanced up at me and said, "Sir, you have learned the name but you do not seem to know to whom it belongs."

I was dumbfounded for a moment and there was silence in the room until broken by the gales of laughter. Then I finally understood that Elizabeth, the daughter, had cooked the meal, not her mother.

But all her brothers came around and smiled and laughed in a most good-natured manner and I knew then that it had been carefully planned as a way to make me feel really part of the family.

Could it be that young Elizabeth is seeking to catch my attention? I wish father or mother were here to advise me in these matters since I know little of them.

Saturday, April 14, 1798

I suppose because she can no longer hide her condition, I was told that Elizabeth's younger sister Sarah is pregnant. It is such an unfortunate condition since Sarah is only twelve. I was not told who the father might be, only that John thinks that Sarah is too young to be married right away. I completely agree with his stance on the matter.

My prayers go out for the child.

Tuesday, July 24, 1798

It is young Elizabeth's sixteenth birthday and I am so fortunate that both she and her family have taken to me so kindly. Every day and in every way, Elizabeth is becoming more desirous as a partner. She surprises me constantly with what she knows and can do herself.

I had made a special trip a few weeks ago to Amherstburg to pick up a small figurine at the general store that I had ordered some months back. It was horribly expensive but I could not help myself.

When I presented my gift to her, wrapped ever so well by the shopkeeper, the entire room went silent as she opened the parcel and pulled out the contents. In fact, for a moment, the silence seemed to be a reproach for such extravagance, but then the gasps of amazement and delight filled in that awkward moment and I knew I had done well.

Tuesday, August 21, 1798

Young Sarah made it through childbirth and she has a fine healthy baby boy.

Once more, my prayers go out for the child.

Saturday, November 3, 1798

News has arrived that the British fleet, under Admiral Nelson, has crushed the French fleet off Egypt. The battle took place last August 1 and has forced Napoleon to retreat back to Italy.

The announcement was made at a township meeting and most of the folk who have settled here attended.

Adding to the excitement over the news from England, I was able to say a few words to young Elizabeth since her family was also present.

Actually, I had a good conversation with her father as well who went into more detail how they fled the rebels in the south and were happy to have found a place here where they could live in peace. I also talked more of my departure from Scotland and how I established a home in Nova Scotia when barely a man with no family upon whom I could depend. He seemed impressed by my fortitude and determination at such a young age.

I was also impressed by the history of the Quick family. John told me how his ancestors had come from Holland and were the first settlers in New Holland. After the British purchased the colony, the family moved to New Jersey on the mainland and stayed there for four generations until the revolution caused them to move again. The rebellion made him and his father nervous of the tyranny of the mob and so they gathered the whole family together and resettled here in Essex County.

It seems that we have much in common, sharing the strength and will to forge new lives out of the wilderness. I like John and see something of a father figure in him. I think he also likes me which is good because I believe I will try to press my suit for his daughter.

I pray God, please give me the courage to do that for which I yearn but for which I have so little knowledge. I really do miss my father and even my brothers at such a time.

Monday, January 14, 1799

It was my twenty-fifth birthday today and Elizabeth came by, accompanied by her two oldest brothers, bringing with them a surprise dinner. In fact, it was a feast and Joseph even brought a bottle of whiskey from the old country. I tried to graciously decline his offer that I should keep the bottle after dinner, but he would not be moved, actually making as if he did not care for the whiskey of the highlands. Imagine!

Elizabeth, bless her kind soul, gave me several pairs of knitted wool socks of which I was badly in need. They were so well done, I simply had to try on a pair there and then. Perhaps the whiskey had some influence as I removed my boots and stockings, but everyone smiled with approval as the socks fit snugly and my boots slid back on my feet making them so very warm again.

She is so kind and, dare I say it, seems to know me now almost as well as I know myself. Even when we are apart for weeks, it is as if we had never parted. Our conversations pick up right where they left off and there are never any of those terribly awkward moments of silence.

What a wonderful birthday it has been!

Wednesday, May 1, 1799

I have found a little clearing far back in the woods where I intend to plant a small flower garden. It is perhaps a foolish thing to do since flowers cannot be eaten nor can they be sold, but I want to surprise Elizabeth from time to time this summer. She will never know from whence they came.

I just heard that John's wife, Elizabeth, is pregnant again. She is due next February. What an amazing woman. This will make eight children but I imagine their last considering her age.

Saturday, September 21, 1799

The summer is done and with most of the work behind us, I got up the courage to ask John if I could marry Elizabeth. After all my worries and rehearsals, he asked me what took me so long!

I have courted Elizabeth all summer by bringing a small bouquet of flowers whenever I travelled to the Quick home. And each and every time I presented them to her, Elizabeth actually squealed with surprise and joy. But today the devil got into me and I purposely kept them hidden until late in the visit when I could see that she was growing increasingly annoyed that I had forgotten to bring any. Even then, she was much too polite to say anything. But as I was about to leave, I brought the ploy to a conclusion by suddenly finding them hidden in my saddle. Her face actually made me think that she might utter a curse on me, but her brothers laughed so hard she could not help herself and finally smiled.

Now that I have John's permission, I will rehearse my proposal to Elizabeth over the next few nights and put it to her next week when I return for Sunday supper.

Sunday, September 29, 1799

She said yes!

Her brothers are so happy for her that they have offered to add two rooms to my cabin as our wedding present. I am overwhelmed and so happy.

Monday, January 13, 1800

What a ghastly shambles. Elizabeth's sister, Sarah, was wed today to Philip Huckleberry. The wedding was planned for last Saturday but due to the horrible weather, it had to be delayed because many of the invited guests had not arrived. My dear Elizabeth was clearly sad to see her younger sister wed before her, but fate played its hand.

Regardless, I care not for the whispers about Jacob, their eighteen month old child. It is the devil's handiwork to see tongues wagging like that. Whatever may have happened in the past is now made good and nothing further should ever be said. For my part, I shall act like they were just blessed with a son shortly after their wedding and patently ignore the reality as any gentleman ought. I am glad to see Philip step-up as a man should.

Elizabeth and I have decided to wait until the fall to get married since that will allow for the completion of the additions to the cabin and another growing season and harvest. It will also permit Elizabeth to be with her mother when her mother gives birth next month.

Thursday, February 20, 1800

Elizabeth has another brother, named Alexander. Both mother and child are doing well. Surely this must be the last child for that poor woman.

Saturday, October 4, 1800

I am writing this in the morning rather than in the evening as has been my habit. I will not have much opportunity later today since I will be wed in a few hours! I am rather apprehensive but Elizabeth and her family seem to be fully supportive. Not having any of my own family here saddens me but her family must be enough for now.

I do not have the best of clothing in which to be wed, but everyone continues to reassure me that it is of little importance. Indeed, most of my friends are happy to see me finally married. I suppose at the age of twenty-six, I should be very happy to have found someone to join with me. It would have been strange indeed to be this age back in Scotland and not already married with several children. But it was important to me to be well established before assuming such a responsibility.

Elizabeth is eighteen and her father seems very happy to see her married before she gets much older. But she has grown into a fine woman in the four years since we first met. She has become very proficient at all the skills necessary to keep a home a welcoming place. She can cook and sew and tends chickens with the best of patience and skill. Most of all, and I am a little shy to say so, her figure has developed into one that seems well adapted to bear many children. I have seen more than a few women suffer through childbirth to want such a fate for her.

But I am getting much too far ahead of the day. I must now get ready to ride to the church.

Part 4: Husband and Father (1800-1812)

Editor's Note

The Historical Context

In Europe, stability did return to France but not in the form that the other royal houses would have preferred. Napoleon Bonaparte relentlessly pursued his ambitions and became Emperor of France in 1804. He aggressively sought to put persons loyal to him and France on the thrones on France's neighbours, Spain and Austria, and even had himself crowned King of Milan. To solidify his empire, he tried to secure the eastern overland trade routes to China and the Far East for France. This would, he thought, cut-off England's trade with the East and weaken her significantly, but he was foiled by Nelson at the Battle of the Nile. Regardless, Napoleon's dominance of Europe was paramount on the minds of the British and the loss of the American colonies in 1776 would have faded in importance compared to the potential for the republican ideas in France finding roots in England.

The Americans were becoming very friendly with the French, and the American expansion westwards as a result of the opening of the north-west territories to settlers was a dark cloud on the horizon for the remaining British colonies in North America.

When Napoleon sold Louisiana to the Americans in 1803 to raise funds for his military, England had two reasons for being concerned. First, it gave the Emperor money to sustain his war machine and second, it looked like a race by the Americans to claim as much of the continent as they could and block the expansion of the remaining British colonies in North American which still provided much needed revenue for England through the Hudson's Bay Company and others.

William's World

But before these grand events took their toll on the Buchanan family, William and Elizabeth started their married life. William detailed his first few married days in rather graphic detail which startled me at first. Regardless of any historical interest, it was impossible for me to feel comfortable reading these most personal entries without feeling like an unwanted voyeur. And while these entries might be of interest to the serious student of interpersonal relationships and other areas of psychology, they have been removed to preserve the dignity and memory of these two fine human beings.

One thing that neither can be, nor should be, hidden is the unconscious male chauvinism that William expresses in many of his entries. In the early nineteenth century, such attitudes were considered normal and even expected. I can only ask that the reader consider the era in which William lived and not judge him too harshly.

I was surprised when I read that two of William's brothers, John and Gordon, also left Scotland for the New World during this period. They were part of Lord Selkirk's Baldoon Settlement attempt. Like William, Lord Selkirk was a native of Kirkcudbright, being born in the town three years before William. The Earl earnestly tried to lessen the suffering of the district's indentured labourers who suddenly found themselves without work or a home because of the new industrial farming techniques. However, as events unfolded, the Baldoon effort was pretty much a failure and most of the surviving settlers left for greener pastures. Gordon moved to Essex County, got married and joined the militia, becoming Sergeant-Major of the First Essex Regiment. William's other brother, John, who was married with six surviving children (his oldest child, John, had died during the voyage from Scotland), moved only a short distance from the settlement to higher and drier ground near current-day Wallaceburg.

Regardless of the Baldoon failure, this part of the diary focuses on the happy and tranquil growth not only of his own family, but also of the families of his brothers and new in-laws. I have to admit that even I got lost amid all the weddings and births that he documented, but these were the things that he missed so badly living alone in Nova Scotia so it is understandable that these are the events about which he would write and find important. To help the reader follow all the people in his life, I have drawn a family tree of William's siblings and in-laws whose names appear in his journal. It can be found on pages 106-107.

Sadly, as the years of happiness went by, the storm clouds of war started to form on the horizon. William seems to have been aware of the darkening future, but I sensed that until early 1812, he really did not believe the Americans would attack. For example, while he made note of the election of the first three American Presidents, he no longer seemed to care when they elected their fourth. To me, that was a sign of how content and idyllic his life had become. He was living his dream and he could not, or would not, allow himself to imagine anything that might spoil it. However, as the threat became more evident, I believe he grew genuinely worried for his home and family, particularly as Elizabeth had been a refugee from the Revolution and her experience would have been a constant reminder of the dangers.

William's Immediate Family

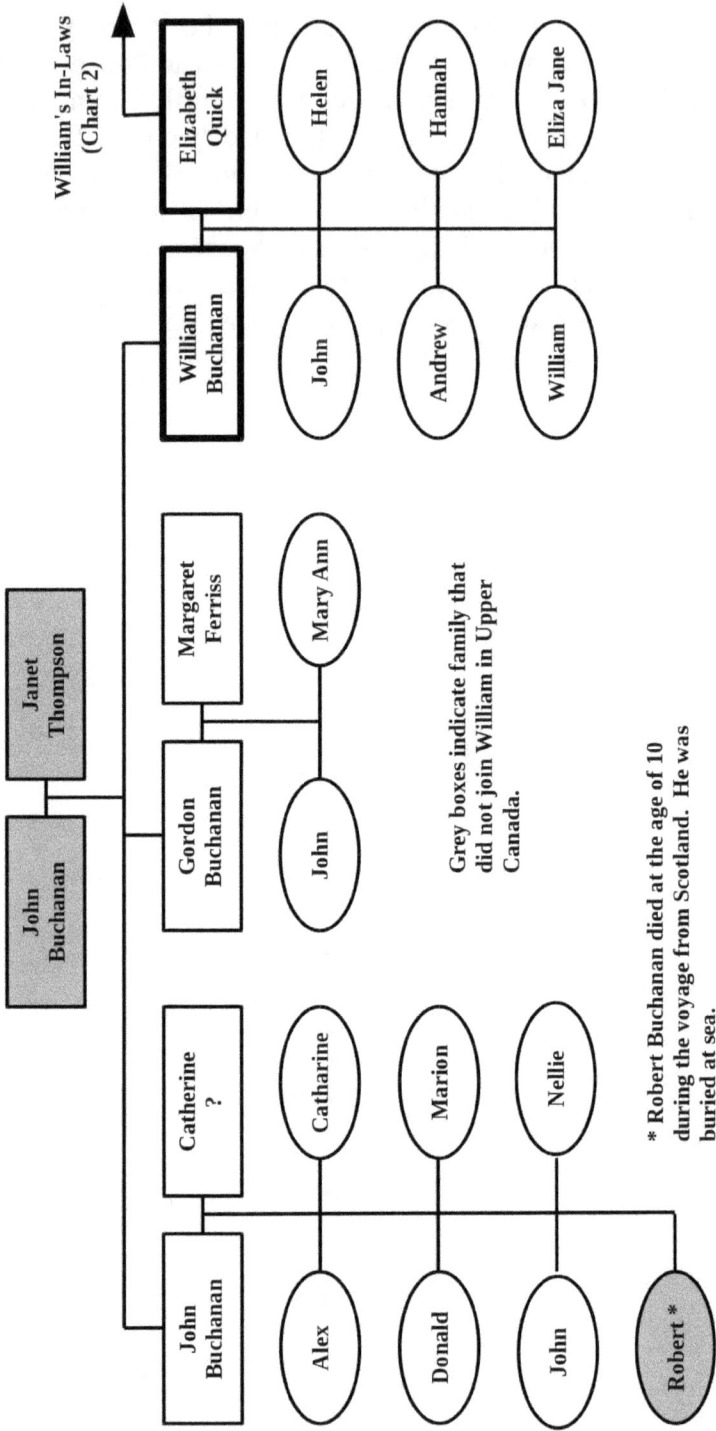

William's In-Laws
(Chart 2)

Janet Thompson

John Buchanan

Elizabeth Quick

William Buchanan

Margaret Ferriss

Gordon Buchanan

Catherine ?

John Buchanan

Helen — John

Hannah — Andrew

Eliza Jane — William

Mary Ann

John

Catharine — Alex

Marion — Donald

Nellie — John

Robert *

Grey boxes indicate family that did not join William in Upper Canada.

* Robert Buchanan died at the age of 10 during the voyage from Scotland. He was buried at sea.

Chart 1

Elizabeth's Immediate Family

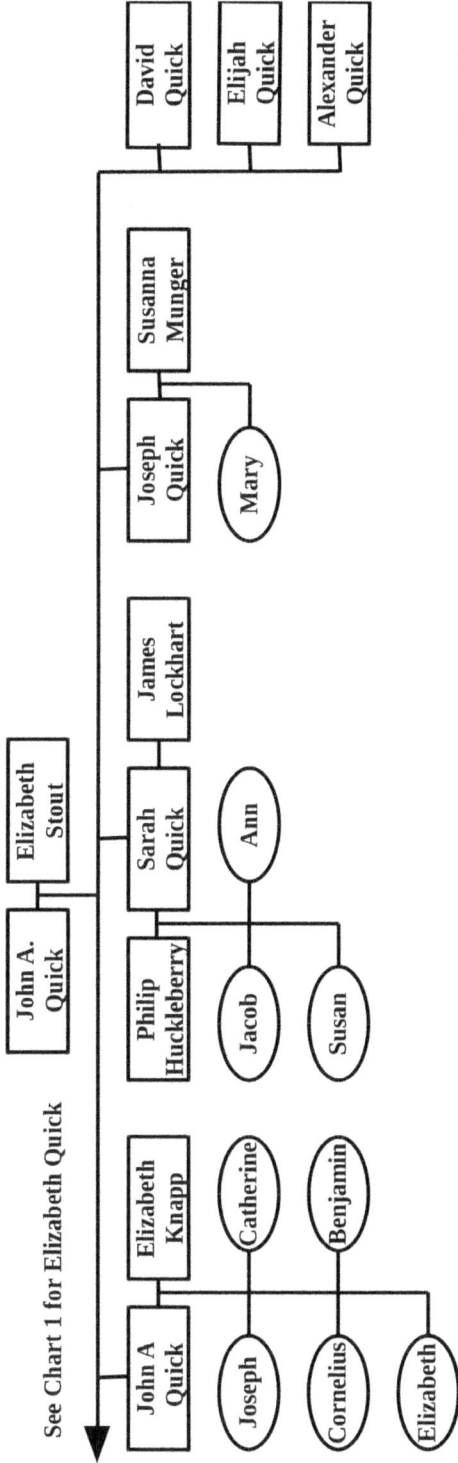

See Chart 1 for Elizabeth Quick

John A. Quick — **Elizabeth Stout**

- **John A Quick** — **Elizabeth Knapp**
  - Joseph
  - Catherine
  - Cornelius
  - Benjamin
  - Elizabeth
- **Philip Huckleberry** — **Sarah Quick** — **James Lockhart**
  - Jacob
  - Ann
  - Susan
- **Joseph Quick** — **Susanna Munger**
  - Mary
- **David Quick**
- **Elijah Quick**
- **Alexander Quick**

Chart 2

107

Monday, October 6, 1800

I must slip away and take some time to catch my breath. Having lived alone since coming to the new world, I knew that the absence of a wife was making my life incomplete. But I can say now that the presence of a wife has made me happier than I think I have ever been.

[Editor's Note: A part of this entry has been omitted to preserve the Buchanan family's memory with dignity.]

I am even beginning to hope for my first son, both to carry my name and to help on the farm.

Life is glorious and I thank the hand of God for guiding me to this earthly paradise.

Tuesday, November 11, 1800

It is Martinmas back home and it is Elizabeth's first opportunity to celebrate it with me as husband and wife. She roasted a huge cut of beef over the hearth for me. I did not ask from where she obtained such an incredible feast, but I suspect one of her brothers put the notion into her head and then either gave her the meat or helped her to purchase it just to please me. It really does not matter how she was inspired or by whom, what is important is that she has been, and continues to be, so very good to me and for me.

Why, I pray, did I wait so long to be married. I simply cannot stop smiling when I secretly watch her doing her chores.

Tuesday, December 16, 1800

Life has broken the spell that I have been under for the past two months.

The recent balloting in the United States has seen Thomas Jefferson elected President to replace John Adams. It is a wonder to me how things can continue to function in a civilized manner with the head of state changing so frequently.

It is also somewhat worrisome because Jefferson is known to wish the English were fully gone from this new world.

Friday, June 12, 1801

Elizabeth prepared an absolutely wonderful supper for me this evening. But there was a method to her deviousness!

She is quite sure that she is with child!

I could barely finish the wonderful repast that she laid out before me for the joy I felt. I am, at last, to be a father! It is late to be starting, but at twenty-seven I am happy beyond words that I will have a son.

Perhaps it is best to say that I will have a child and not jump to any unwarranted conclusions, but I am sure in my heart it will be a boy!

Wednesday, June 17, 1801

Apparently, the United States declared war last May against the Barbary pirates in the Mediterranean. Such nerve! How can they conduct a proper war that far away and under the noses of both Napoleon and Nelson.

Does this mean that they intend to challenge the great European nations for a position of power and influence? Surely, their hubris shall lead them to ruin.

Wednesday, September 4, 1801

Elizabeth's sister Sarah gave birth to a second child two days ago. It is a girl and they have named her Ann. Mother and child are doing well. Elizabeth's mother was there and becoming quite the expert mid-wife.

I am now an uncle twice.

Friday, December 25, 1801

Elizabeth and I had decided some time back not to make the trip to her parents for Christmas because of her advanced condition. Thus we were surprised when her mother and father and two oldest brothers appeared with everything prepared to eat.

It was wonderful to see Elizabeth's family doting on her in such a way. I think they are as anxious as I am for this birth. Elizabeth's mother will return when the baby is close to being due to help out.

Sunday, February 7, 1802

What a momentous day! I became the father of a healthy baby boy early this morning. Elizabeth struggled, but her mother was here and both Elizabeth and child are doing well. Since Elizabeth's father and my father were both named John, the choice of my son's name is without doubt.

I have to admit that I sometimes wonder about our Good Lord's judgement giving women the burden of childbirth. How could He, in His grand design, make our women suffer so. I suppose I was naive, but I always thought that hitting my thumb with a hammer was wickedly painful. Today, Elizabeth has shown me how petty my own discomforts have been compared to what she has endured.

On a brighter note, this being February, she will be up and doing her chores well before the winter is over. I playfully scolded her about laying in bed for so long when there was plenty of work to be done. She did not reply, but when her eyes fixed on mine, I felt the malice and said nothing more.

I must write to my father with the wonderful news. It is another event for which he can be proud of me.

Saturday, May 8, 1802

Elizabeth's younger brother, John Alexander Jr., got married today. It was a splendid wedding with spring having arrived early. The sun shone brightly and everyone was captured in the moment. I understand that his bride, Elizabeth Knapp, is only seventeen while he is twenty-seven. But their age difference is not that dissimilar to the difference between Elizabeth and me. Therefore, I am quite sure they will be very happy.

Elizabeth's sister, Mary is due to be married next month so we shall have to gather together again very shortly for more joyous celebrations. I suppose work will get done sometime between these family affairs.

Saturday, June 12, 1802

It was Mary's turn today to be wed. She married James Ramsay, a good and hearty fellow that has lived here most of his life. I do not know much of James' background, not even how old he is, but I suppose such things are of no matter provided he is good to her and her to him.

Thursday, September 2, 1802

The heat and humidity have been oppressive all this summer but I now know that John was right when he said that corn grows best in this sort of weather. The rains came when they were needed and the crop has grown tall and heavy with many cobs on each stalk. I hope that the crib I put together will be big enough to hold all that has grown.

I borrowed John's wagon to bring in the second cutting of hay which has dried nicely in the sun. I will take the wagon back tomorrow and then ride home.

Sunday, January 30, 1803

Elizabeth's brother John and his wife Elizabeth have been blessed with a boy for their first child. His name will be Joseph.

John is walking around so tall, one might think that he was the one, not Elizabeth, who bore the child. But I shall forgive him since I know what a proud moment this is for him.

Friday, April 8, 1803

The territory to the south of Lake Erie, called Ohio, has been declared a full state of the United States. They gained statehood last March.

This cannot bode well. Surely, the Americans have rushed Ohio to become a state to lock in their claim to that land.

I fear the Americans are coming ever closer to us and I pause to think how far things will go.

Friday, July 22, 1803

At supper tonight, Elizabeth told me that she believes that she is pregnant again. She hopes that it will be a girl but I am firm that a second son will be of more use in the coming years as work on the farm grows.

She grew rather silent at my admonitions and then I realized I needed to gently restate my hopes simply for a healthy child and uneventful birth. Marriage does seem to have its challenges after all.

Wednesday, August 17, 1803

News has arrived from England that the Americans have purchased all the French territory called Louisiana from Napoleon. The agreement was signed last April. It is unknown how much they paid the French, but this means the Americans are serious about blocking our growth westwards.

It is of concern as well since that money will be used by Napoleon to further his European ambitions.

It is most worrying that these European disputes seem to be creeping ever closer. I cannot help but think that the Americans have changed their mind about assisting the French against the King.

Saturday, October 15, 1803

I received a letter from Scotland today. It held wonderful news! Two of my brothers, John and Gordon, have decided to come to Upper Canada and settle nearby on land that Lord Selkirk has had set aside for them. John is bringing his entire family, including his wife Catherine and his seven children, none of whom I have ever seen. Gordon is not yet married but decided his fortunes lay in the new world as mine did.

They will be arriving sometime next year and will be settled at a place that is no more than thirty miles to the north-east of my own home.

I cannot wait to introduce Elizabeth and my son to them!

Tuesday, March 15, 1804

What a blessed day! A second son has been safely delivered to Elizabeth and me. We will name him Andrew after his uncle, my beloved brother, who still lives in Scotland.

My brother Andrew was born two years before I left home and is the only other brother I have known. After I left, mother and father had a girl, Helen, and two more boys, John and Gordon, both of whom I shall see for the first time in a few months.

Would it not be a joyous day should the rest of the clan decide to join Elizabeth and me in this great land of unlimited promise. Alas, such an event is a foolish hope as I cannot imagine my parents contemplating such an arduous voyage at their age. Therefore, I must resign myself to the notion that I shall never see them again. That makes me rather sad.

But I must chase those sad thoughts away and be joyful for today is a day to truly celebrate.

Saturday, August 25, 1804

This was to have been such a wonderful day, but a great sadness has overshadowed my joy.

John and Gordon arrived this morning at Amherstburg and I was at the dock with Elizabeth, John and baby Andrew to greet them. While Gordon is alone, John introduced me to his wife, Catherine, and their children. I had expected to meet all seven of his children, but poor little Robert perished on the voyage before they made land in Newfoundland. What should have been a joyous reunion instantly became melancholy. Despite their loss, John and Catherine are determined to make a go of it and I admire their courage in the face of such a terrible tragedy.

We did not have long to hear John and Gordon tell stories of father and mother, nor for them to listen to the adventures I have had. After only a few hours, they were off again by small boat up river to Lake St. Clair and then to the Chenal Écarté where Lord Selkirk has obtained land for them. Each family will eventually get fifty acres of their own.

I could not bring myself to speak of it, but I have heard that the land to which they are headed is rather marshy and not very well suited for farming. But surely the Earl must know what he is doing.

In any case, I am so happy to have family here, even if they will be a week's journey away. That is a mere pittance compared to the ghastly Atlantic.

Friday, November 9, 1804

Sad news came by post today. Elizabeth's grandmother on her mother's side, Ruth, passed away some six weeks ago in New Jersey.

She lived to the amazing age of ninety-five. As Elizabeth would have me believe, her grandmother was just too stubborn to have died any earlier. Ruth's husband, Benjamin, passed away in 1767 and when the family decided to leave New Jersey after the Revolution, she absolutely refused to go with them since she wanted to be buried beside her beloved. Now she has her wish and they will be together for eternity.

Sunday, March 18, 1805

Another planting season is almost upon us and I have much for which to be thankful.

I have two strong sons and now, in addition to Elizabeth's family, I have my own kin living not so very far from here.

Despite the dense hardwood forest that grows here, I have cleared nearly 20 acres since first arriving nine years ago. The land is rich and I have been able to plant corn, wheat and hay, not to mention the garden vegetables for our own table. I have a tool shed, corn crib, and a small barn for the horses and our two cows. I have struggled but managed to put together several good sturdy chairs, a table where we can share our meals, a hardy cradle for our youngest and a large bed for the boys in the other bedroom. I am still not certain what we shall do if Elizabeth finally gives birth to a girl, but I will deal with that when and if the time comes.

I have noticed how each fall, countless geese and ducks appear from the north and rest nearby before flying across the lake. When my aim is good, they make a wonderful source of fresh meat for our table.

If I have one complaint, it is the ever present swarms of mosquitoes in the summer. Some folks seem to be immune, perhaps because they taste bad to the insects. But I cannot seem to escape them and become consumed with the destruction of each and every one of them, just as they are consumed of me.

In the end, I suppose, it is a small price to pay for the many blessings I have received. So I shall just try to bear their ceaseless attacks since they too are God's creation. Could it be that He created them as a means to temper our sinful pride?

Tuesday, June 4, 1805

Word arrived today that the authorities in York have become very serious about the establishment and maintenance of a militia in Upper Canada. I was not even aware that in 1793 an act was passed requiring all men between 15 and 50 to register and serve. Nor was I aware that a year later the upper age was pushed to 60 because there were not enough men who registered in that first year to adequately defend the colony. It seems that even here most of the local men simply ignored the call to arms and none were ever sanctioned for it.

I fear, however, that the times have changed. It is rumoured that the English are becoming more apprehensive of the Americans since Napoleon sold the entire Louisiana territory to our southerly neighbours.

The authorities want to establish at least one regiment, and perhaps two, to be based at Fort Amherstburg.

Of course, I cannot ignore such a call to arms. Thankfully, Elizabeth is fully supportive of my decision. She does not wish to see our peaceful land taken by the republicans to the south.

I will journey to the fort next week to sign up and learn all that may be required of me.

Friday, June 28, 1805

My stay at the fort was longer than anticipated but for good reason and with good result.

Because of my age, being thirty-one now, and my sea experience, the garrison commander has decided that I shall be commissioned a Captain in the First Essex Regiment and lead a company of men to be trained as marines. This is a great honour and responsibility.

From time to time, perhaps twice a year, I will gather together the local men who have also enlisted so that they may practice their gunnery and other military disciplines. One of the regular officers from the fort will join us during those exercises to impart his expertise.

Imagine me, a Scot, not only in the English army, but an officer to boot!

Saturday, August 10, 1805

Gordon has written to me about the sad situation of the Baldoon settlement. He tells me that Lord Selkirk has asked that they move to higher ground to avoid the unhealthy marsh conditions in which they now live. Gordon does not know if Mr. McDonnell[13] intends to honour the request from his Lordship, but I hope that he does for the well-being of all the settlers.

Wednesday, April 30, 1806

Elizabeth is quite sure that she is pregnant again. Her being with child will again interfere with the growing season but I cannot blame her entirely. Still, I will have to be a little more circumspect in future to avoid such a conflict.

Thursday, May 1, 1806

All of the men who enlisted in the militia from this part of the county gathered to take part in their required military training. Major Reynolds arrived yesterday to oversee the training and offer assistance. He is a fine gentleman with a strict but fair demeanour.

We will gather like this twice a year from now on until the militia is no longer needed.

Friday, December 12, 1806

My brother-in-law, John, and his wife Elizabeth have been delivered of their second child, another boy. At least John is not so swelled this time and I am very happy for them both. He says they will name him Cornelius after his grandfather.

Sunday, January 25, 1807

Our third child came into this world today and it is another boy! I convinced Elizabeth that he should bear my name, William.

Her mother stayed with us again but will leave early tomorrow. She says that Elizabeth is well versed now in taking care of herself and with a son going on six and a husband, she did not feel her presence was required. I have to admit, she is looking a bit tired and so I do not begrudge her leaving so soon.

Tuesday, February 3, 1807

It has been a grim day. Elizabeth's oldest brother, Joseph, rode by to deliver the news that their mother passed away sometime during the night.

I cannot imagine into what torments Elizabeth's soul must be sinking particularly so soon after the birth of our third child. Does she blame the burdens that she put upon her mother for her mother's sudden demise?

When Joseph finished speaking, Elizabeth was very still but then, very slowly, she stood up from her chair and thanked Joseph for taking the time to come himself with the news. A tiny smile graced her ashen face and both Joseph and I could see she was fighting the pain. He repeated how sorry he was about having to be the bearer of the news.

Elizabeth reached out her hand to take his and then put her other hand on top of both. She thanked him again through ever more cloudy eyes and then she asked if he would like to stay for supper. He glanced quickly at me and I shook my head. Reading my thoughts, he muttered something about having to tell their other brothers and sisters the sad news. Then, realizing his words carried possible offence, he mumbled something about what a good cook Elizabeth was and perhaps another time would be better. With that, he moved to the door with a couple of quiet steps, said his farewells and was off.

Even then I knew that Elizabeth could not have taken such news so calmly and with such grace. For my part, I found words impossible and I was shaking inside, barely able to contain myself.

And true to my thinking, as soon as Joseph closed the door behind him, I watched as Elizabeth sank back into her chair as slowly as she had risen. But when her body came to rest, her head continued downwards slowly, inch by inch, until it rested in her hands on the table.

It was then that she began to sob in a most pitiful way.

I tried my best to console her but I think these things just have to take the time needed. She insisted on telling the boys herself, alone, saying something about women being better at explaining such things and it was, after all, her mother that had passed. So when the boys came in from their chores, I slipped quietly into the bedroom and listened. Blessings be on her soul as she sat and talked to the boys with the same composure and grace as she greeted the news initially. While I listened, my hand reached for the drawer where I had carefully hidden the bottle of whiskey Elizabeth's brother had given to me. I saw my hand do it, but there was such an emptiness in my soul that it did not seem real. When I poured a wee drop into the small silver dram cup father had given me just before sailing and raised it to my lips, whispering Elizabeth's name, the taste of the whiskey brought me back to the bitter reality of the day.

We must start planning the trip to the funeral. The children have not really had death come so close to them and I pray that my shoulders can bear both their fears and Elizabeth's sorrow until, like all things, those feelings fade into the past.

We men must remain the pillars of stability in such times of deep sadness.

Thursday, October 1, 1807

The men of my militia company gathered again for our second drill of 1807. They do not need much practice with their muskets since all seem to be good shots. But the Major reminded everyone that loading their guns and shooting while under enemy fire is a very different thing.

I have no doubt he is correct.

On a brighter note, I received a letter from Scotland today that carried with it news of my brother Andrew's wedding to Helen Cannon and of my sister Helen's wedding to David Rae. Both weddings took place last June and both couples are now happily living in wedded bliss.

That leaves only my brother Gordon as unwed.

Thursday, October 22, 1807

Elizabeth is with child again. But she is not quite as excited as before. She misses her mother greatly and this will be her first birth since her mother's passing.

She has told me that she hopes this child is a girl in memory of her mother. I neither can, nor wish to, argue the point with her.

Wednesday, December 2, 1807

Elizabeth's father, John, seems to be coming around out of the melancholy state he was in following his wife's death last February. Indeed, he introduced me to the widow, Mary Squire, who lost her own husband not so long ago. It would seem that the two of them are getting along very well and I certainly cannot blame John for seeking companionship.

I shall have to see how my Elizabeth takes to this lady.

Saturday, April 23, 1808

I rode to the Fox farm to help them put up a shed. When I arrived, he had already dressed and stacked the logs and I have to admit that I felt a little ashamed for not having done the same back when the neighbours arrived to help me raise a new shed.

Then I saw his secret. He owned a grind stone mounted on what looked like a small spinning wheel and was able to sharpen his adze and two-handed planer frequently thereby making short work of those logs.

Because of the work he had already done, it took no time at all to put up his shed. We were done well before supper but the women insisted we stay to eat before going home. They were obviously grateful for the help and I was glad to have repaid some of the kindness that has been shown to me.

Sunday, June 19, 1808

Finally, Elizabeth has delivered a baby girl! But I have begun to wonder about so many children born on Sunday. I hope that our Dear Lord will not be annoyed at Elizabeth's labour on the Lord's Day. Elizabeth wishes to name her Helen.

Sunday, July 3, 1808

Elizabeth's father was re-married today to the widow, Mary Squire. His new wife brings with her a ten year old daughter, Mary, from her previous marriage so Elizabeth now has a new step-sister in addition to her new step-mother. I am happy for John and his new wife since they can now rely on each other rather than both being alone in this wilderness.

Thankfully, my Elizabeth has quite taken to her new step-mother, a turn of events for which I am grateful.

Monday, December 12, 1808

I am an uncle again! John Jr. and Elizabeth have been blessed with a lovely daughter.

He has told me that Elizabeth is firm that their first girl should be named after herself and he is in no mood to argue the point. From my own eight years of married life, I completely understand.

Thursday, June 29, 1809

Once again, Elizabeth is pregnant. At least she will not be so uncomfortable over the summer this time. She would like another girl and I do not wish to argue with her but I would not mind another boy.

Saturday, November 18, 1809

I heard some dreadful things about the Baldoon settlement today. There have been many deaths and it would seem that Alexander McDonell, the man who the Earl put in charge, has been making a right mess of things. I hope that both John and Gordon are doing well and, if not, that they will consider moving closer to us here where things are so very good. I could not bear the thought of having to write father and mother if something horrible happened to either of them.

At least his Lordship has had the good sense to dismiss Mr. McDonell before all is lost.

Friday, January 31. 1810

Elizabeth's brother John and his wife have had another child, a second girl. Some time ago, they had settled on the name Catherine if the new arrival was a girl so I assume that is what they will name her.

I wonder if John wants to have a larger family than Elizabeth and me. Perhaps I should ask my wife about her brother's ambitions.

Thinking more about it as I sit here, it may be best that I just keep silent.

Monday, March 12, 1810

I have another daughter! And I think that Elizabeth took it to heart about so many births on Sunday so she had the good sense to hold on one more day. We will name her Hannah.

Wednesday, April 25, 1810

My brother Gordon got married today to Margaret Ferriss. She is nineteen and was born in the North-West Territories of the United States. But she has chosen to leave that country and make her home here with Gordon. Cheers for her!

Added to our family joy, Gordon has decided to move and settle here in Essex County and has already signed up for the militia. I am so proud to say that he is to become the Sergeant Major of the First Essex Regiment. Gordon has become such a fine gentleman.

Sunday, May 20, 1810

It is only two months since Elizabeth was safely delivered of Hannah and now she tells me that she is pregnant again. I think this is too much for her to bear and perhaps this should be our last child. I dare not speak to her of this now, but I shall wait until this child is born and have a very serious talk with her. At thirty-six, I am getting too old for this.

Saturday, June 16, 1810

Elizabeth's oldest brother, Joseph, got married today. Joseph is five years older than Elizabeth and looked every part the gentleman. He married Susanna Munger whose family also fled the American Revolution.

They have both waited a long time to get married. He is forty-one and she is said to be thirty-nine. Clearly they will not enjoy a large family! But it is good that he is finally settling down and I wish him all the best.

Friday, November 9, 1810

I am honestly beginning to have trouble keeping track of all the children brought into this world by my wife's siblings.

I heard today that Sarah and Philip have had a third child, a girl that they named Susan. Mother and child are said to be doing well.

It being only another six or seven weeks until Christmas, my mind has formed a vision of all these excited nieces and nephews in one place. Please let it not be so. What utter chaos it would be.

Of course, I know in my heart that it is a blessing to have so many healthy children in the family and, thinking back, this is the very thing for which I yearned when I felt so desolate in Nova Scotia. Just please let them not all clamour about me at once.

Friday, January 4, 1811

Very sad news today. Elizabeth's sister, Sarah, lost her husband earlier today when his musket exploded while he was hunting. It is doubly hard knowing that Sarah just gave birth to their third child less than two months ago. Elizabeth has been tearful most of the day wondering how her sister will manage on her own with the three young ones.

But as Elizabeth is seven and half months along with our own child, I have convinced her not to come with me to the funeral. I will offer condolences from the both of us. I am sure Sarah will understand.

Sunday, February 24, 1811

Elizabeth has delivered another girl, and on Sunday again! Now we have three boys and three girls all of whom are healthy and completely wonderful. We will name this latest addition Eliza which is a shortened version of Elizabeth. My wife did not want any of her children to bear such a common name as her own.

Tuesday, May 21, 1811

What a beautiful spring day, doubly blessed by two wonderful pieces of news.

My brother Gordon and his wife Margaret have a healthy baby boy! I know exactly how he must feel and I wish him and his new son every happiness in this world.

And there are even more glad tidings!

Elizabeth's brother, Joseph, and his wife, Susanna, have been blessed with a new daughter. They told me some time ago that if they had a girl, they would name her Mary.

Since Elizabeth has tried to assume much of the responsibilities that her own mother used to shoulder, she is busy packing to lend her brother a hand until Susanna is up and about.

Saturday, November 9, 1811

Well, it was not long that Elizabeth's sister, Sarah, remained a widow. She is now safely remarried to one James Lockhart. I am sure he is a most honourable gentleman, but it is less than a year after Philip's terrible accident which seems a bit soon for her to be wed again.

Still, life must go on and the children will now have a father again.

Thursday, November 14, 1811

News has arrived from Amherstburg concerning an American attack on an Indian settlement at Tippecanoe. An Indian runner brought the news of how the American governor of the Indiana Territory organized a force of settlers and slaughtered the villagers without mercy. According to the runner, the attack took place a week ago on November 7. Those that survived saw their possessions and winter stores put to flame and there is great fear that they will starve over the coming winter.

I am beginning to fear that our semi-annual militia training may be put to use sooner than anyone had hoped or imagined.

I pray for the sake of our family and the families of Elizabeth's brothers and sisters that the Americans become content with what they have and do not continue to press so recklessly forward.

Friday, February 7, 1812

John had his tenth birthday today. I am so proud to see him grow and fill out. Soon he will be a man just like his father.

I sat down with him by the fire and told him how my father, his grandfather, had apprenticed me to a captain sailing for the New World when I was his age. And I talked about how I made my own home first in Nova Scotia and then later here in Upper Canada.

He kept looking at me with eyes as large as saucers but seldom interrupted save for a few simple questions. He is such a good listener and learner.

In a way I am thankful that he does not have to set out alone across the vast ocean to become a landowner and gentleman. I am sure he will find other tasks to test his mettle.

Friday, May 1, 1812

As he has done so many times before, Major Reynolds arrived yesterday to supervise our semi-annual training exercises. They have become rather routine, but all of us sensed something different in the Major.

He tells us that the Americans have become much more friendly with the French and there is serious talk abroad about how they (the Americans) could help their new friends by attacking the colonies here. It is thought by the French that such an attack would divert men from Europe and thereby make England weaker on that front.

I had not paid much attention when the Americans elected yet another person, James Madison, to be their President in the autumn of 1808, but perhaps I should have. He is known to have a great dislike for the Indians who, he believes, must be pushed aside for the benefit of his country.

And if the whole truth were known, I think he and the American people would also very much like to see England off the continent.

Oddly, everyone seemed affected by the Major's thoughts and, as a result, this was a day of earnest training without much of the ordinary conversation that used to be the norm.

Friday, May 15, 1812

Major Reynolds stayed behind after the training had finished. He sat down with me and, while Elizabeth prepared some food, he told me that most of the officers at the fort believe that war is inevitable.

Much to my dismay, Elizabeth overheard his assessment and dropped a large cast iron kettle filled with her wonderful soup. She begged the major to say it was not true or that the odds favour peace. But he reluctantly confirmed his earlier statement.

I cannot allow Elizabeth to become despondent not only for her own sake and mine, but also for the sake of the children. I tried to re-assure her that we were more than capable of withstanding any foolishness on the part of the American army or navy, since we had superior numbers and armaments on both land and water.

But despite me listing all the ships we have at our disposal and how well made and armed they are, all she could see was the danger to us and to the children.

I pray that war does not come.

Part 5: Soldier (1812–1813)

Editor's Note

The Historical Context

These are William's war entries and they mark his final days. I felt an enormous sense of sadness reading them for the first time. One can feel him changing from proud victor to a person barely hanging on to life for the sake of his family.

While the British eventually prevailed, not only against the American invasion of their remaining North American colonies, but also against their main adversary on the European continent, Napoleon, it is doubtful that William could even have imagined such an outcome. He died during the blackest days of the war when it must have seemed a hopeless cause.

The colonies emerged from the war stronger and more determined than ever to remain apart from the American experiment. Indeed, following the war, the dream of a flourishing British North America was pursued with even greater vigour by, among others, Lord Selkirk who finally achieved success and a place in history for his support of the early settlement of Manitoba.

Lord Talbot also stepped up to finish the road that he had started before the war. It loosely followed the Lake Erie shoreline, linking Fort Erie with Sandwich. Talbot had seen it as necessary to cement the colony from east to west and, had it been built a few years earlier, it might even have saved Fort Amherstburg and William.

While the British held off the Americans, it is hard to argue that the Americans actually lost the war since they did not have to give up anything of significance in the treaty that followed. Therefore, since neither was defeated, both sides claimed victory.

Perhaps the only real losers were the aboriginal peoples who failed to realize Tecumseh's dream of an independent nation-state on North American soil. Indeed, the fortunes and influence of the first nations steadily declined in the years that followed and remained bleak until modern times. Now the courts have become the First Nations' principal ally in support of their historical land claims.

William's World

William's diary habits changed dramatically during this period, writing something almost every week, and often every day.

He did this once before when moving from Nova Scotia to Upper Canada, but during that trip he was likely bored and had little else to do.

These war entries, though, reflect something other than a man bored. I believe they reflect a man who is apprehensive of an uncertain future but determined to do his best as an officer to defend his home.

The reality of warfare in William's time mostly involved two lines of men marching toward each other, halting when they were perhaps only a hundred feet or less apart. Then both sides would raise their loaded muskets and, on command, fire them at the enemy opposite. Men would fall on both sides, but then the lucky ones who were not shot would be ordered to reload and both sides would fire again. The whole process took real courage and discipline to stand and take the enemy's fire without breaking rank and seeking shelter. It is little wonder that desertions were common among the militia and William's company suffered like all the others. Fortunately, most of the men who deserted from his Company in the early days of the war returned to duty and fought as honourable men for their homes and families.

I did not research how many men in William's company were lost, nor how many fled and never returned to duty. To my mind, it does not matter after two hundred years except to some academic studying the war. It is enough for me that William stood up for what he believed and died in support of that cause.

I truly wish William could have seen something of the future country that he defended with honour. At the very least, I wish he could have lived to see his family not only survive the war, but flourish after the occupation. His third son, William, achieved the rank of Captain in the militia following in his father's footsteps and lived to see the colonies enter Confederation in 1867.

It is the cruelest of ironies for a soldier to die knowing only that the cause for which he has fought and suffered seems to be lost and then, after his death, to have fate turn around and bring victory to his side.

All wars are an irrational failure of human beings to live together in harmony and sharing. This war was no different. The global ambitions of men like Napoleon and President Madison conflicted with the entrenched privileged nobility of Europe and the resulting antagonism resulted in the death of thousands of common men across Europe and North America. William became one of those casualties simply trying to defend that which he had worked so hard to achieve.

Tuesday, June 30, 1812

This morning, a courier from Fort Amherstburg delivered a letter from Colonel Allen. It is war! The Americans declared war on England on Monday, June 15.

The Colonel has ordered me to gather the men of my company and make haste to report to the fort as soon as possible. There is some concern about the American forces at Detroit.

Elizabeth is naturally worried but is holding much of that in reserve for the sake of our older children who understand the seriousness of the situation. John is now ten and Andrew is eight. How fast the years go by.

I have sent John to spread the news and to ask the men to gather here quickly, as early as the day after next if possible. If everything goes well, I am hopeful we can depart for Amherstburg on Friday.

Most of the men in my company are my neighbours and friends. They are all good men but I know that they must be worried about the future, as am I.

Friday, July 3, 1812

Some of the men have arrived but not all. Since I do not wish to split the company, leaving someone behind to gather the stragglers, we must postpone leaving.

My son told me that many of the men wanted to attend services on Sunday before marching to war, which is perfectly understandable although ill-timed. That being the case, therefore, I do not believe that we will be assembled and ready to depart until Monday morning at the earliest.

Monday, July 6, 1812

We began our march shortly after enjoying a last meal together with our wives and children. They all gathered to wish us God speed and victory. I know that the march will take us more than a few days since we have to carry so much with us and the trails are not that well marked. It also slows us down when we have to make and break camp each day. Thank goodness for the long hours of daylight.

Sunday, July 12, 1812

The company finally reached the fort this morning. It was a long trek from Gosfield but it seems we have arrived none too soon! Word has been received that the Americans have crossed the Detroit River and are preparing to march south to attack the fort here. Under the circumstances, even our small numbers could make a difference so our arrival was greeted with enthusiasm by Colonel Proctor and the other troops.

Although General Hull's aggressiveness is worrisome, I am encouraged by our good fortune to date. Just nine days ago, on the third of July, my good friend, Lieutenant Roulette, was on board HMS General Hunter when they spotted the American vessel, Cuyahoga, sailing up river to Detroit. With all the bravado he could muster, he got the Captain to launch him and several others in a long boat and, with one shot from his pistol, he managed to capture the ship! According to him, the American captain did not even realize that war had been declared.

Even more fortunate was the fact that among the vessel's cargo was a crate containing the personal papers of General Hull, the commander of the Detroit garrison. I am told that the documents revealed a treasure of information about American troop strength in the area and how the General intended to begin the campaign. While we must assume that he will now reconsider those intentions, it has given us a glimpse of his way of thinking which will, I'm sure, be a great boon to our cause particularly now that he has taken the offensive.

Monday, July 13, 1812

I am ashamed to say that before starting our march north, six of my men failed to answer muster this morning, presumably preferring the safety of their farms to the uncertainty of confronting the enemy.

The river is still running strong from the spring thaw and so we were caught off guard by the American general's bold strategy. They have no significant naval strength to support their attack and that leaves them vulnerable if our ships stop their supplies from crossing the river. In fact, Colonel Proctor has ordered parts of our fleet to proceed north to the mouth of the River Canard so they can bring their cannons to bear on the American troops.

Indeed, our naval superiority was enhanced today when the schooner, HMS Lady Prevost, was commissioned and joined our fleet. I am particularly anxious to get on board to see her for myself. She will, no doubt, be an asset in the coming days despite her untried crew.

The only enemy ship of any note that might be capable of causing us alarm is the brigantine, Detroit. She is now anchored at the settlement for which she is named. However, she would be foolish to sail down river to attack us since we would be able to answer her fire with a far superior force. Therefore, it is more likely the Americans will use her guns to anchor their defence as they launch their invasion.

Tuesday, July 14, 1812

Nine more men failed to answer role this morning but we continued northward. While my company is not alone to suffer such shame, I am deeply worried about our future since such actions can drain the morale and determination of the entire company. Indeed, Colonel Proctor met with all the regimental officers to express his displeasure at the number of desertions and it was not pleasant.

To lessen the effect that these disappearances have had on the company, I have spoken to the men in an effort to maintain their resolve in the face of imminent battle. I have also prayed most earnestly that we succeed in this, our first engagement.

Wednesday, July 15, 1812

Eight more men quietly disappeared last night.

Word has it that we will finally meet the enemy tomorrow and I have grown to believe that it cannot come soon enough because it is the unknown that makes men fear.

Sleep continues to come with great difficultly, so I walked among the men this evening speaking to them with as much confidence as I could muster hoping to bolster their morale and to deter more absences.

No one knows what tomorrow will bring, but I believe that God is on our side and will not let us be defeated.

Thursday, July 16, 1812

It has been a horrible day. The Americans defended their position with exceptional strength and our own men broke when the enemy counter-attacked. We did, however, manage to re-group and retreated in an orderly manner south. Thankfully, and somewhat mysteriously, the Americans did not pursue us. I wonder why they did not press their advantage?

Although our first battle was not a success, at least I can take solace knowing that only two men failed to report after the battle. More importantly, no one from my Company was struck down and for that I am most grateful.

Our ships are sailing up river but have been slowed by the current. Despite that, they should be in position to provide supporting fire by tomorrow. Perhaps the Americans fear our naval guns and that is why they have not advanced any further. It is also strange that the Americans did not deploy any of their artillery during today's battle. Perhaps they either lacked the boats to move their cannon across the river or they feared that our ships might sink them.

Saturday, July 25, 1812

Word has arrived that our troops have captured Fort Michilimackinac in the north! That is the first bit of good news in several weeks.

Colonel Proctor has decided that instead of attacking the American positions up river, we should instead strike out across the river to the west and south-west and harass their supply routes from Ohio. At least this is far better than sitting around at the fort worrying about the enemy positions to the north. Proctor also thinks that General Hull, the enemy's commander, may become concerned about being trapped between us and our troops in the north at Michilimackinac. Let us hope the Colonel's ideas bear fruit.

Thursday, August 6, 1812

An Indian runner arrived today with news of a skirmish at Brownstone, not far inland from the western shore of Lake Erie. He told us that a small force led by Tecumseh himself routed a much larger force of Americans, numbering perhaps two hundred, with few casualties to themselves and several dozen American troops killed.

This is good news indeed since it ought to worry General Hull even more that his supply lines cannot be maintained. It remains to be seen, however, if it will embolden him to some rash action or make him more nervous and thus more cautious.

Sunday, August 9, 1812

Most of the men who deserted the Company last month have returned from their farms and again reported for duty. I am most grateful for that. Rumours abound concerning the arrival of additional regulars to reinforce the garrison here and it would not do us any good to be seen as lacking the character to defend our own homes.

Ensign Stockwell, two sergeants and eighteen privates have not yet returned. Nevertheless, I remain hopeful that they will rejoin us in due time and, in doing so, not further embarrass themselves and the Company's honour.

I was particularly pleased to see Elizabeth's cousin, Cornelius, back with news of Elizabeth's well being. I understand that he spoke to many of the men who had left and bolstered their resolve to return. He will, no doubt, inspire the men by his courageous determination to defend his home and this land. He is at heart a truly honourable man and is an asset to the Company because of his formidable accuracy with a musket.

It is also good to see all four of the Fox men reporting back. They have put every male member of their family in service and their renewed resolve is remarkable.

I would like to discover if the other companies have fared as well with their returning recruits. I want to express my pride in the men, but before lauding our own returns, I think it would be best if I discretely try to learn how the other companies have fared so that my pride cannot be mocked.

Monday, August 10, 1812

Major Muir has returned from another engagement with the Americans south of Detroit near the Indian village of Maguaga. The troops, with assistance from a good number of Tecumseh's warriors, did not achieve the same degree of success as at Brownstone, but they did face a much larger American force of more than five hundred men with cannons.

Regardless, our men did inflict at least two dozen deaths on the enemy for only one man lost on our side. Further, Muir has confirmed that the American column turned around and went back to Detroit from whence it came.

Their retreat would seem to indicate a pattern of not pressing home any advantage. Perhaps the Colonel is right that they lack the determination to really pursue this war to victory. If so, that is very good for our collective futures.

Thursday, August 13, 1812

General Brock arrived by boat this morning bringing with him a large number of regulars who were a welcome sight. Apparently, he navigated westwards along the Lake Erie coast, absent any significant escort, so as not to attract the enemy's attention.

The General wishes to immediately deploy the new troops to re-take Sandwich.[14] He is certain the Americans who are still encamped there can be driven out quickly not only because of our overwhelming advantage in men but also because they are unaware of the reinforcements he has brought.

Once Sandwich is secured, he wants us to immediately move our cannon to positions opposite Detroit and make them ready to bombard the town and fort by that evening. Then, under cover of darkness the same night, the General plans to cross the river with the main battle force and complete the envelopment of the enemy's fort before dawn. Clearly, he greatly values the element of surprise and believes that our speed may lead to swift victory in this battle. Needless to say, we were all impressed with the boldness of his plan and the confidence with which he explained it to us.

As the battle plans were detailed by the staff officers, I learned that my men will be spread throughout the fleet to provide for its defence and, if it is subsequently determined that they are not required in that role, we will join the main assault force as reserves.

Asking us if we had any questions, but barely waiting for anyone to speak up, the General lowered his voice and began to speak about how this would be the first major engagement for most of the men and he expected his officers to be vigilant and disciplined in the face of the enemy. He turned to the militia officers and repeated how he wanted us to maintain the strictest discipline in our men. I felt a little shiver run through my body but I knew my responsibilities and girded myself for what was to come.

Having now met our commanding general, I feel compelled to write down my impressions of General Brock. He is a most striking figure, being well over six feet in height with a handsome face that demands attention. If there is one small flaw in his appearance, it is his girth. Perhaps the General eats too well between battles.

In truth, he is only five years my senior, but he has had some remarkable adventures. He even served with Lord Nelson at Copenhagen and, after the battle, dined with his lordship in celebration of the Admiral's triumph.

Surely with such a man in command, our fortunes are assured.

Saturday, August 15, 1812

Wonderful news! Our assault on Sandwich has driven the enemy out and we have moved our guns up so that they are within range of Detroit. We began the bombardment late this afternoon.

At the same time, General Brock and Chief Tecumseh convened a staff meeting to confirm our plans to cross the river. When the meeting began, the General honoured me by most graciously requesting that I should interject should they appear to be making any ill-founded assumptions about the river crossing.

He confirmed his intention to cross the river tonight and begin the assault against the fort at first light. I could see on the faces of almost everyone there a certain unease, and even fear, concerning the great haste with which Brock was moving. In fact, only Tecumseh expressed his unreserved support for Brock's plan and praised him for his warrior spirit. Seeing the other faces around him, the General explained, once again, the value of surprising the Americans before they had time to discover how the balance of force had changed and noted in particular the caution with which General Hull had conducted operations on this front to date. Our commander pointed out that in battle such caution can often lead to indecisiveness when the unexpected happens thereby paralyzing the enemy and permitting us to overwhelm them before they can regain their senses. Brock's lecture on military tactics had its desired effect, calming the faces in the hall and with that he adjourned the meeting, wishing us all good fortune in the battle tomorrow.

The regiments have all been ordered to board the ship, or ships, to which they have been assigned and, with the late summer decline in the current, it should not be difficult to get them all across before dawn.

Once again, I am having trouble sleeping but I must put the pen down now and try to get some rest before tomorrow. The men are counting on me.

Sunday, August 16, 1812

Oh what good fortune fate has delivered! Without firing a shot, General Hull has surrendered Detroit!

He was awoken to the sounds of drums, both of our own and of Tecumseh's braves, and the marching boots of nearly two thousand soldiers. I have never witnessed such a force. Our ships were positioned off-shore and the regulars and militia, along with the Indian warriors, were well placed to launch the attack before the Americans even seemed to be aware of us. I, myself, was on board the Queen Charlotte, a sixteen gun sloop, and was anxiously waiting to hear her cannons roar. However, it was not to be.

While I am confident we could have taken the town with a minimum of effort, General Hull feared for the safety of the civilians under his care and in a gentlemanly and honourable gesture negotiated the surrender without jeopardizing their safety.

Nevertheless, we are victorious! And this victory puts an end to any American plan to cross the river again as they did last month.

When we dined this evening, General Brock and Tecumseh both praised the troops for their discipline and fine showing and we raised our glasses in tribute to the General's boldness and success.

Before putting down my pen, I must comment on Tecumseh's command of our language and, indeed, the eloquence with which he spoke. He is wholly committed to pushing the Americans out of the north-west and restoring the lands that they have taken from his people. I am comforted in knowing that the Indians are not our enemies to be feared, but rather our allies in this war.

Monday, August 17, 1812

At a staff meeting this morning, General Brock indicated that he would be returning to the Niagara frontier almost immediately. He will be leaving Colonel Proctor in charge and, in fact, gave the Colonel a field promotion in honour of his new responsibilities.

Sunday, September 6, 1812

With the American threat now much lessened, General Proctor has given permission for many of the militia to return to their farms to ensure the crops are harvested before the frosts come. I myself will take some time to return home to Elizabeth to make sure all the preparations for winter have been made.

But more importantly, my brother Gordon has announced that his wife is pregnant again. Of course, that means he will receive a discharge from the militia within the next few days to return to her until she safely delivers. And who knows, perhaps this war will be over before that blessed event.

Monday, October 5, 1812

After spending a couple of weeks back home making sure everything is in readiness for the winter, I am back now at Fort Amherstburg. I am content that Elizabeth, with the help of John and Andrew, will fare well over the coming months.

My boys have made me so proud, rising up to the challenge of managing the farm in these difficult times. They are truly a joy and comfort to me.

General Proctor has decided that we will prepare for an aggressive defence of this western-most frontier against the Americans. He wants us to work on plans for harassing the American troops between here and the Ohio frontier so that they cannot establish a reliable base from which to launch an attack against us as they tried to do last summer.

It is hoped that the river freezes early so that we can ferry our men and supplies by sledge rather than by boat. That would make things much faster and easier. But we will have to wait until well after Christmas before the weather becomes suitably cold and the ice thick enough to support our sledges.

Tuesday, October 20, 1812

Dreadful news. Word has come that, although General Brock led our troops to victory at Queenston Heights a week ago, he was struck down during the battle and lost his life.

It was widely rumoured that the King would almost certainly honour him with a Knighthood and other titles in recognition of his capture of Detroit. Now, I suppose, those honours will have to be posthumously granted. For my part, I am thankful to have spent several days in his company, a time that I shall never forget.

Nevertheless, his loss is truly a grievous one. Chief Tecumseh is visibly sad. He respected the General for taking the war to the Americans and for his promise of setting aside territory in the American north-west for a true Indian nation. One must hope that Tecumseh's determination to see this war to victory does not suffer.

But the General is gone now and we shall have to forge ahead in honour of his memory.

Monday, November 2, 1812

The first snow has fallen and the temperature has dropped quite suddenly. It is unusual in my experience to be this cold so early but the Indians all say that they expect a much colder winter based on the signs they have been reading. Let us hope they are mistaken.

Sunday, December 13, 1812

It will not be long before Christmas is upon us but Chief Tecumseh is determined to press the enemy whenever and wherever they can be found. His scouts have returned with stories of an American build up in Ohio that they say is meant to re-take Detroit this winter. I cannot imagine a worse time to be marching north from their barracks but perhaps that is precisely how they expect to achieve surprise.

Tecumseh himself will leave the fort shortly with a band of warriors to head south along the western shore of Lake Erie to search for these rumoured troops. At dinner tonight he proudly explained that if he found such a force, his warriors would deliver a mighty reminder that these are the lands of his ancestors and that his people shall not be removed from them.

Wednesday January 8, 1813

The General has ordered my company to set out across the lake to support Tecumseh's men who believe that a march by the Americans northward is imminent. Since the mouth of the river and the lake are not yet frozen over, this should not be a difficult exercise. Several other companies and some regulars will also travel with us.

Can one dare to hope that the Americans will once again surrender quickly as they did in Detroit or will they bring a greater resolve with them this time.

Wednesday, January 20, 1813

Tecumseh's scouts were correct about the American's intention to launch an offensive this winter. Indeed, his scouts have reported that the Americans are now less than a day's march from our current position.

Forewarned, we have established a line just north of Frenchtown completely hidden from the Americans who continue to advance unaware of our presence. Tecumseh is supremely confident of his warriors ability to attack even in this cold weather and that confidence is spreading among the regulars and militia.

My own men have not engaged the enemy since Detroit, a battle which did not materialize and was not, therefore, a great test of their mettle. That means I must keep my eyes and ears open for any signs of weakness in their ranks. I could not bear the shame of so many desertions again.

Friday, January 22, 1813

We have won a great victory at Frenchtown thanks in no small part to our Indian allies under Tecumseh. General Harrison, for whom the Indians have a great hatred because of the slaughter at Tippecanoe, tried to move a large force from Ohio north along the western shore of Lake Erie in an attempt to retake Detroit. But the Indian scouts gave us ample warning and we laid in wait for them.

Quite a large number of the enemy were killed and even more surrendered. We will have to deal with those prisoners somehow. I suppose we will have to march them east through Upper Canada to York or even further to a more secure prison facility. I am very glad to be with the Marines and thus not subject to this kind of duty.

I had a chance to overhear some of the American troops. They are mostly from Kentucky and have an equal distrust, even hatred, toward the Indians and Tecumseh in particular. It seems that they blame him for the many raids on their frontier settlements.

Saturday, January 23, 1813

Sweet Lord above, how I wish this day had never been. Some of Tecumseh's braves found themselves alone with the Americans and proceeded to perform unspeakable acts upon their persons. Very few were left alive and those that did survive were mostly taken away by the Indians as their slaves. I cannot imagine a worse fate.

I am absolutely sure that Tecumseh would never have allowed this, but he left the battle site last night to return to Fort Amherstburg. There was no one who could stop the Indians from exacting their revenge and taking, as they put it, trophies.

The carnage was worse than the battle yesterday. I cannot bring myself even to describe some of the acts perpetrated on the Kentucky men. I have seen cannon and musket fire tear a man's flesh, but this went beyond.

At least those men will not have to endure long years of captivity in prison, but I cannot think that will be much comfort for their widows and children.

As we no longer have any prisoners to move or guard, we will be returning to Amherstburg tomorrow. General Proctor would like to gather his staff together to discuss our next manoeuvres.

Sunday, February 21, 1813

The General stated this morning, in no uncertain terms, that he wants to avoid the failure of discipline experienced at Frenchtown and wants us to plan a more conventional campaign against the very base of American operations in this region.

We know that General Harrison has spent a great amount of time and effort fortifying the Ohio-Michigan border and it is there that he continues to receive reinforcements. Most of his new men are from Kentucky which baffles me because I do not understand why they are so motivated to wage war against us. Some say it is because they wish to end the Indian threat to their homesteads by defeating Tecumseh, but surely they could achieve peace at far less cost simply by treating the Indians fairly. Still, even if they were motivated thus, why would they direct their aggression against the settlers here with whom they are likely to have much in common.

In any case, the winter has been harsh, just as the Indians predicted but it will end just as surely as it began. And when it ends, we must set out again to forestall any American attack on our homes.

Sunday, March 14, 1813

We have completed our planning for a major assault against the Ohio frontier but we must wait now for the river and lake to become ice free. Spring, it seems, does not wish to arrive but the days are now becoming longer and there have been a few warm days. Spring will officially arrive next week and we are all anxious to bring the war back to the Americans.

Friday, April 23, 1813

Our ships are loaded and we are ready to sail tomorrow for the Ohio frontier. Let us hope the weather will be kind and the winds fair.

This will be our first great battle under General Proctor. To date, the Americans have shown no great will to press home the war and have, in fact, shown a reluctance to put up a real defence. We are filled with hope, therefore, for another great victory as was had at Detroit last summer.

Monday, April 26, 1813

We landed at the mouth of the Maumee River having crossed the lake unopposed. We possess a great force complete with regulars and our Indian allies. The cannons have been disembarked and we will begin the march up the river to Fort Meigs in the morning.

Saturday, May 1, 1813

Our twelve and twenty-four pounders began the bombardment of Fort Meigs this morning. But we were surprised by the new mud fortified walls. Those walls are absorbing our cannon fire very effectively. However, we will continue to bombard the fort in the hope that our artillery will eventually have an effect.

Wednesday, May 5, 1813

A large force of Kentucky soldiers moved out of the fort to attack our cannon positions and, most unfortunately for us, they succeeded in their objective.

But having accomplished this minor victory, the Americans decided to press their advantage only to fall into a trap set by Tecumseh's Anishanabe warriors. The Indians slaughtered almost the entire enemy force of 800. Tecumseh is beaming with pride for his allies.

Since this engagement took place away from the enemy fort, the General has started to refer to it separately as the Battle of the Miami and greatly praised the Indians.

But I have heard that Tecumseh was not as enthusiastic about General Proctor. When the General witnessed some of the Indians executing prisoners from the battle he did not interfere but reproached Tecumseh for his braves' behaviour. Tecumseh retorted that the General, having been there, should have exercised his authority and stopped them himself. Rumour has it that Tecumseh muttered something about Proctor not having the courage to interfere, or something similar in meaning in his native tongue. If true, this does not bode well for future relations between us and our native allies.

Sunday, May 9, 1813

With the loss of our heavy cannons, General Proctor has decided to disengage the enemy and return to Amherstburg.

While we did not take Fort Meigs, the elimination of the Kentucky troops can be considered a major victory. It will surely blunt any offensive plans that General Harrison might have had.

Sunday, May 16, 1813

In the middle of this horrible war, there is a bright note today. My brother Gordon has been blessed with a baby girl. She was born on May 3 and has been named Mary Ann.

I pray that the war does not find its way to his home so he can watch his two children grow as I have been able to do with my own. It is an evil time but the Lord has still bestowed a joyous blessing on Gordon and Margaret.

Monday, June 6, 1813

General Proctor has ordered us to draw up plans to attack Fort Meigs again this summer. He is convinced that if we can take the fort and then demolish it, we will have dealt the enemy a blow from which they are unlikely to recover for another year. He wants to meet again next Monday to discuss our recommendations.

Although we did not succeed in our first attempt, it is hard to argue with his logic and how serious a blow it would be to the enemy, but I think that the fort will prove just as tough to assault as it did two months ago.

I must think hard about what can be done. If I can identify even one weakness in the enemy's fortifications perhaps it could be the difference. But their fort looked very well built and I have no doubt that the enemy troops have been encouraged by our failure to take the fort in May. It is always more difficult to defeat an enemy whose morale is solid. If we assume that they will not make the same mistake of over-pressing any tactical advantage as they did before, then we will be faced with a most difficult challenge.

Monday, June 13, 1813

A large number of options were discussed today, none of which really sounded that much different than our first attempt. Despite that, General Proctor believes that if we can achieve surprise by attacking the same target again so quickly after our initial assault then we ought to have better fortune. He is firm in his belief that the Americans can be dislodged from Fort Meigs and that the destruction of their fort is our best hope to blunt any offensive plans they may have.

I am not sure how I feel about the plan upon which the General settled. Having now experienced a number of battles, I am left rather apprehensive about this one.

But I have faith that our cause is just and that, with God's help, we shall prevail.

Sunday, July 4, 1813

The Americans are busy celebrating their independence from England today so we have taken the opportunity to load much of the required arms and supplies onto the ships that will carry us across the lake. It is hoped that, because of their celebrations, no one will notice our preparations from across the river and send word to Ohio.

Saturday, July 10, 1813

We had hoped to set sail today but there are ominous dark clouds on the horizon and with the oppressive heat and humidity that seems to haunt this land with some regularity, it is most likely a severe storm on its way. I have found that summer storms here can be very destructive with high winds and even hail. It is not a time to be on the lake.

On a more base level, I am once again being consumed by a plague of mosquitoes. With all our other concerns, what moved our Good Lord to create such monsters? They are so numerous this summer, they threaten to hide the moon behind their black swarms. Everyone is slapping and scratching.

Wednesday, July 14, 1813

We landed in Ohio this morning, close to where we landed just two months ago. We disembarked the troops and guns and then began the march inland back to Fort Meigs. Everything depends on our achieving surprise so we are being very cautious and avoiding any drums or other loud noises.

Tuesday, July 20, 1813

This has been a very bad day. General Proctor had put much stock in the value of surprise being on our side. But earlier today a small group of our men was discovered and only three survived to return with this grave news. Our surprise is no more.

But I still have faith that we will prevail. Our force is probably the largest we have ever assembled against the enemy, being close to five thousand men if one includes Tecumseh's warriors. Surely, the Americans cannot withstand us now since they cannot hope to receive any reinforcements in time to help their cause.

Monday, July 26, 1813

This has been a day of confusion and I fear that our strategy may have to be changed before this battle is done.

Tecumseh's warriors staged a very noisy mock battle to draw out the American troops, but for some mysterious reason, they remained behind their stockades and did not take the bait.

Please let this not be a sign that they have learned of our plans.

Tuesday, July 27, 1813

It is becoming evident that the Americans will not be lured out of the fort to do battle. Indeed, it has caused the General to become increasingly worried that the enemy had foreknowledge of our plans and may have already set in motion a force to cut us off from the lake and any retreat.

Still, we continue to exchange fire with the enemy but I think the General has lost faith that we can win this battle.

Wednesday, July 28, 1813

I am writing this entry despite the constant pain from the wound I received earlier today. It is helpful to put my mind to another task so as not to dwell on my misfortune.

I simply cannot believe that a simple farmer from Kentucky was lucky enough to put a musket ball into my leg from that distance. But I suppose those are the fortunes of war.

The medic has offered me great comfort and assures me that I will be fine in due course. I would not dispute his professional opinion, but I have seen lesser wounds take many a man away from this life. Regardless, I must put such thoughts far from my mind and trust in his judgement because I am experiencing a great desire to see Elizabeth and the children again. I promised to come home with victory assured.

At least I did not have to march back to our ships. Instead, I was carried by litter to the lake shore where I was taken aboard HMS General Hunter which will sail for home in the morning.

At this very moment, I cannot imagine returning to a more desirable place.

Sunday, August 1, 1813

The surgeon, Doctor Eberts, removed the ball from my leg yesterday but the pain was so great as he dug it out that I lost consciousness. I suppose it is no great shame to have passed out, but I had hoped to set a better example for the other men who were to have shot removed from their bodies after me.

Doctor Eberts has a great deal of military experience having served with the Hessian troops during the revolution to the south. I am in the most capable of hands.

Major Reynolds was kind enough to inform me that a courier has been sent to tell Elizabeth of my plight. I do hope she does not worry or tell the children. In a few weeks all will be back to normal and any such worries will have been a complete waste of energy.

Monday, August 9, 1813

My leg has swollen in a most disagreeable manner and a fever keeps returning. The good doctor has spent many hours at my bedside and I feel that he should be devoting more of his time to the other wounded.

He raised the unthinkable today. He suggested that to combat the infection he really ought to remove the leg. I told him that I could not consent to such a radical solution without talking to my wife.

But this fever sometimes makes it impossible to know what day it is and if anyone has been to visit. The courier brought back a note from Elizabeth that she would try to visit sometime this week.

I must force myself to be alert, calm and re-assuring when she is here. I cannot let her see me in delirium.

Sunday, August 15, 1813

I am so ashamed of myself. The doctor told me that Elizabeth was here on Friday but I have only the most hazy memories of her presence.

She did leave a note that is more comforting than any medicine the Doctor pours down my throat. She is so sweet but reminded me that the crops will need harvesting so I must get myself better and out of bed soon.

The good Reverend Pollard who is the fort's chaplain paid me a visit and we spoke of many things but I fear that I tested his patience as I went on and on about my children. I have become almost consumed with the desire to see them all again. The Reverend says that is just the Lord's way of confirming that all will be well.

The Reverend also asked if I had thought about my leg again. Without thinking, I spoke to him rather sharply with a tone that I now regret.

Monday, August 23, 1813

The new American fleet, launched from Presque Isle earlier this summer, has sortied out onto the lake. They did so after Commander Barclay had to lift his blockade of the enemy's home port a few weeks ago due to his supplies running low.

At first the American ships appeared to be headed for Amherstburg, but turned back to a port in Ohio without engaging our fleet. I am not surprised since I cannot imagine that their fleet could be any match for the Royal Navy.

Nevertheless, I am stuck here when my company is making ready to sail with our ships to sink this American nonsense to the bottom of the lake where it belongs. Why can my body not heal itself.

Saturday, August 28, 1813

I continue to lose track of the days because this fever will simply not relent except for brief spells such as now. I think it is the twenty-eighth day of August but I cannot be sure. I must ask one of the medics and correct my date if I am wrong.

At least I am alert enough to notice the great preparations of the fleet that will be leaving harbour shortly. My hopes and prayers are with them even if I cannot be.

Saturday, September 11, 1813

I feel dreadfully weak but I must write down just a few words.

It is almost unimaginable but our entire fleet on Lake Erie has either been sunk or captured by the Americans off Put-In-Bay, Ohio. Commander Barclay returned late today and I could hear him relating how Commander Perry, who was in command of the American fleet, graciously allowed him to keep his sword after he surrendered on HMS Queen Charlotte. At least there is some chivalry among the Americans.

But I just do not understand how this could have happened. When the American fleet left port after we lifted our blockade and dared to sail west to the mouth of the Detroit river, they seemed to lose their nerve and turned back. To me it was obvious that they had no stomach to pick a real fight with the Royal Navy.

So Barclay, having re-supplied our ships, set out to catch the Americans and teach them a lesson. And indeed, as the battle began, our superior gunnery showed and the American flagship, the USS Lawrence, was disabled and eventually sank. The American commander was even forced to transfer his flag.

Then, by some inexplicable and curious twist of fate, fortune turned against us and we now find ourselves bereft of any naval force protecting our supply lines.

It is now more urgent than ever that I get better and go home to Elizabeth and the children. I fear the coming weeks.

Tuesday, September 14, 1813

This fever will not leave me and it is only tonight that I have enough strength to write a little more in my diary.

The doctor sent a courier to Elizabeth asking that she come and visit before the end of the week. He included, at my pleading, the thought of bringing the two eldest boys. I do so want to see them again. John is now eleven and Andrew is nine. They are fine boys of which I can be proud. They are taking care of everything in my absence and I feel so guilty for it.

However, I am fearful that the good doctor's urgency either means that he wishes to press more forcefully to remove my leg or that he now anticipates the worst. Still, my faith is strong that I shall survive this crisis and go home to my Elizabeth and our children. I have not come this far over ocean and continent to be stopped by some accidental misfortune.

Thursday, September 16, 1813

I am feeling very melancholy. Since the loss of the fleet, everyone here is anxiously waiting to hear from General Proctor concerning what is to become of our fort and us. Surely without a fleet on the lake to protect our supply ships, we are in a most precarious position, worse even than General Hull's position in Detroit at the start of the war a year ago.

My doctor continues to smile and remains optimistic despite what appears to me to be worsening symptoms. I am writing this entry during a period of relative lucidity when the fever that haunts me has relented for a time.

Elizabeth is due to visit tomorrow and I am hoping to be in good spirits for her. It is a long trip and I want to present myself in the best way possible for her. I am not sure if she will bring any of the children because it is just too perilous for them. Still, to see John and Andrew would bring cheer to my heart.

I will pray for their safe journey, and the benefit of her wise council regarding the leg.

Editor's Postscript

That was William's last entry. He died three days later on Sunday, September 19.

His death left me with so many questions. Did Elizabeth arrive on that Friday and, if she did, did she bring their two eldest sons? Did William remain lucid enough to greet her and calmly discuss his precarious state? If the boys were there, did he have a chance to say what he wanted to say to them?

If William was unable to make an informed decision because of his illness, I wonder if Elizabeth, desperate to save his life, authorized the amputation? And if so, did the surgeon attempt it and did William die as a result of the surgery? Surgery at that time was brutal in the absence of any anaesthetics and would have been even more risky considering William's condition.

On the other hand, if William was alert and lucid, was he too proud to accept what fate had dealt him? Was his stubbornness, or as other Scots might say, his determined resolve, both his greatest strength and his ultimate failing?

There are so many questions that cannot be answered. The only clear fact about his death, other than the date, is that Elizabeth did get to Fort Amherstburg in time to recover his possessions including this journal.

By mid-September, as William fought for his life, the fort was in a state of chaos and its English commanders seemed powerless to restore calm.

Succumbing to the chaos, General Proctor decided, only days after William's death, to abandon and destroy Fort Amherstburg to avoid it falling into the enemy's hands.

However, in a desperate last-minute attempt to keep the British from leaving, Tecumseh made an impassioned public plea to General Proctor to rescind his orders and stay to defend Upper Canada. Using particularly strong language, he essentially accused Proctor of cowardice in the face of the enemy. Proctor's decision, and Tecumseh's angry reaction to it, set the stage for Tecumseh's last two battles. Keeping to the rear of the British who were retreating up the Thames valley, he fought a delaying action at The Forks (now Chatham) with only token British support. But that action was insufficient to stop the Americans and Tecumseh decided to fight them again fifteen miles further upstream at Moraviantown, close to today's Thamesville. That was where Tecumseh fell and, with his death, his dream of a nation-state for aboriginal people in North America faded into history.

Despite Tecumseh's failure on the battlefield, the Americans did stop their pursuit of the British, not because of any military threat but because of their own supply problems. General Harrison had wanted to pursue Proctor all the way to York, destroy the English army in Upper Canada and thus "liberate" it from British rule. But supply issues plagued him just as they did General Hull and General Proctor. So the Americans returned to Amherstburg and settled into their new base, Fort Malden, determined to protect their gains. They would occupy that part of Upper Canada for the next two years, giving it back only in 1815.

It may seem a stretch of logic to attribute the end of the aboriginal dream of an independent nation-state located in the American North-West Territories to Proctor's decision to abandon Amherstburg, but that decision certainly set in motion the events leading to Tecumseh's death and no First Nation leader has ever come closer than he did to making it come true. Of course, whether an independent nation-state could actually have been realized given the militant and determined expansionism of the Americans is a moot point, but those few weeks remain a defining moment in First Nation history on this continent.

General Proctor did not escape criticism by his own people for his decision to retreat, and faced a board of enquiry to answer for it. In retrospect, it is hard to imagine any other choice he could have made since he had been completely cut off from supplies over Lake Erie by the American fleet. Still, it seemed to many a rather defeatist and even cowardly thing to run in the face of the enemy and so he suffered the consequences.

I am still left with one final but important question. Did my great-great-great-great-grandfather really make a difference in the War of 1812?

We should all remember that every soldier who serves makes a difference, some in large ways and some in not so large ways. William was an officer and a leader of his men. As such he helped to win the early battles but then lost his life at a time when the war must have seemed to him a hopeless cause.

To conclude that he was merely a minor player who made no difference would be to offend every serving soldier in every country in every war since such things began. One of the biggest differences between the common soldier and the generals who command them, is that the little people who actually give their sweat and blood often end up being swept from history as if they were just dust.

The monuments erected to the great generals serve a purpose, but we must never forget that without people like William, wars cannot be fought, let alone won. Our remembrance of each and every one of them is the only way we can ever repay the great debt that we owe them. No common soldier has ever died, or will ever die, in vain.

Footnotes

[1] There were no passenger ships in the eighteenth century. But it was common practice for ships to allow individuals to book passage for themselves and their possessions. However, this did not include meals. Passengers were expected to provide for themselves as required.

[2] Beltane was celebrated on May 1 in Scotland with the lighting of bonfires. It marked the time that the cattle were put out to pasture from the winter barns. It was also celebrated by the baking of oatmeal cakes.

[3] Halloween was not celebrated in the eighteenth century. Instead, All-Saints Day was celebrated on November 1. In addition, the Gaelic holiday of Samhain was also celebrated on November 1. Samhain was marked by selecting the farm animals to be butchered and generally celebrated the harvest time.

[4] Lammas is the celebration of the new wheat crop and one of the Scottish "quarter days". The quarter days were days when contracts could be signed or terminated, including personal services such as maids, butlers, etc.

[5] In the old English currency, "1/-" meant 1 shilling and 0 pence. Amounts less than a shilling were written as "6d" for six pence. There were 12 pence to a shilling and 20 shillings to a pound.

[6] The last Scottish rebellion had been in 1745 when "Bonnie Prince Charlie" had attempted to restore the Stuart line to the throne of England.

[7] President Washington was keen to stay neutral since he did not believe the United States would be able to exert a military force of any consequence and he did not wish to become entangled in European affairs.

[8] Upper Canada had been divided into districts and later into counties. The Western District included the modern counties of Lambton, Huron, Middlesex, Elgin, Kent and Essex.

[9] The Battle of the Plains of Abraham was fought on September 13, 1759. William was a little off on his arithmetic since it was nearly 40 years earlier, not 30 years.

[10] Newark was the capital of Upper Canada until 1797 when the capital was moved to York to be further from the American border. Newark was renamed Niagara in 1798 and then Niagara-on-the-Lake in 1970.

[11] York is now called Toronto.

[12] Martinmas was originally the feast of Saint Martin of Tours and became one of the Scottish quarter days.

[13] Alexander McDonnell was hired by Lord Selkirk to manage the settlement but spent most of his time in York pursuing his own business interests rather than looking after the settlers. As a result, many of them suffered and some lost their lives. Finally, after repeatedly ignoring the many suggestions Lord Selkirk made to improve the settlers' lives, McDonnell was sacked by the Earl in 1809.

[14] Sandwich is now Windsor.

Appendices: The Real Facts

Appendix 1:

An Homage To Two of My Ancestors

I am a writer. I never used to call myself that, but looking back maybe that was always my vocation, hidden under other titles and ambitions. Most recently, I have written and published my own auto-biography and a series of philosophical essays based on my life's observations. Nearly 40 years ago, I ended my academic career by writing a Master's thesis. Between those events, I have written constantly, producing technical manuals for computer systems, white papers for government operations, and project proposals seeking millions of dollars in funding.

My thesis was completed using an IBM Selectric typewriter. Many readers may not know what made the Selectric a great leap forward in office equipment, and if they are under thirty they may not even know what a typewriter is. The Selectric was revolutionary in its day because it allowed the typist to change fonts on the fly by means of small interchangeable balls with raised type-face to strike the page. My own Selectric, despite being an early model, made me the envy of every other graduate student and I made some money on the side by allowing others to use it. But typewriters are not word processors. In those days, spell checking was done using a large heavy physical dictionary, referenced because of an uneasy gut feeling that the word you had typed, or wanted to type, might not be correct. Grammar was something that you had to remember from dreadfully boring lessons in high school or face ridicule from your peers and bosses.

Today we no longer need to be experts at either spelling or grammar since the word processing software on our computers instantly spots potential inaccuracies and helpfully suggests alternatives. However, two little problems remain with the technology. First, when the software offers a number of suggestions, the author still needs to recognize the correct one to select. Furthermore, the software is still too dumb to recognize when a perfectly good word is not the one required or intended.

Modern communication providers have built their business models around charging for time used on the network and therefore treat the required hardware and software as commodities to entice customers. That means when customers send text messages, it is in their own self-interest not only to shorten phrases into acronyms but also to shrink words into single letters or numbers to match the sound of the word being replaced. It is a nifty time and cost saving trick developed first by a few clever individuals and then adopted by millions.

There are lessons to be learned here.

The first is that time brings change, even to language, so we must all adapt. Trying to stop evolution is just not possible.

But there is also a more subtle lesson that some may have missed. Technology used to be a force that made our lives easier. Now, it has evolved into a force that is changing the very way we live. It is demanding that we learn new tasks and skills and our dependance on its capabilities leaves us little choice but to conform. Humans would face catastrophe on a scale unimaginable if just one modern invention, the electricity grid, were to be cut off for even a few weeks.

Two hundred years ago, people survived based on their wits, their physical strength and simple durable technology. To the Europeans, North America was still a vast wilderness sparsely inhabited by indigenous peoples. In fact, it seemed a perfect place to exercise their self-reliant determination in an effort to prosper beyond anything possible in the old world.

When examined from the perspective of the First Nations though, it was the beginning of the end of their ancient way of life. Even the simple technology imported by the Europeans, foretold doom for those who chose not to adapt or conform. It is a lesson that needs to be remembered in our modern society.

Quite a number of my ancestors were pioneers in Southwestern Ontario. Some of them were among the first to clear the land on the north shore of Lake Erie in what is now Essex County. Furthermore, I was pleased to discover that, despite the vast cultural gap, they co-existed peacefully with the local aboriginal tribes, some of whom had traditionally inhabited that area and some of whom had migrated there from the United States after the Revolution.

At that time, my home town of Chatham was called "The Forks" and the Thames River was called Rivière La Tranche. Along that river, the Crown set aside large tracts of land for the Ojibwa and Iroquois people who had been displaced by the Revolution. The aboriginals had their own name for the Thames River, calling it the Askunessippi. To the west of the Thames valley, along the south shore of Lake St. Clair and on the eastern banks of the Detroit River, there were a number of Wyandot settlements that had existed for many generations.

The relative peace that existed between Upper Canada's early settlers and native peoples did not exist to the south of the border. Tensions continued to grow, particularly in Kentucky and Indiana after the American Congress opened the Northwest Territories for settlement in 1787. The Northwest Territories stretched across the area of present day Ohio, Indiana, Michigan, Illinois and Wisconsin. While there had been hostilities between natives and settlers for a number of years in Kentucky, the relentless American expansion westwards eventually lead to more widespread and deadly confrontations. The celebrated Battle of Tippecanoe in 1811, led by Governor Harrison (later President Harrison), was really a military slaughter of an entire native settlement based on American fears that the natives would hinder their growth. That action pushed many tribes to ally themselves with the British Crown in the war which was to start a year later. It has, in fact, been argued by a number of historians that the cumulative effect of the American expansion by force was to build the reputation of Chief Tecumseh and his efforts to define and declare a sovereign state for indigenous people on roughly the same land that the Americans had opened to settlers. Tecumseh understood that the beginning of the nineteenth century would probably be the last opportunity for native people to shape their own destiny in North America before losing that chance to the swelling invasion of Europeans.

The British, after their ignominious defeat by the forces of the thirteen colonies along the Atlantic coast, became determined to keep the northern part of the continent under their rule. Therefore, a sort of arms race began in the late eighteenth century with fortifications and

227

naval ships being constructed to defend the Great Lakes and Atlantic regions. At the same time, Britain was being challenged by a mortal enemy across the English Channel where Napoleon had assumed power after the French Revolution. For the British, it must have felt like their future was under the most serious threat since the Spanish Armada.

When my great-great-great-great-grandfather, William Buchanan, set out across the Atlantic, I doubt that he had even the slightest idea of the watershed epoch into which he would find himself thrust.

He fled the reforms that were pushing people off the estates they had worked for centuries, immigrating from Scotland first to Nova Scotia and later to Upper Canada. Being a land owner and a member of the gentry in Scotland would have been an impossible dream for people like William. Land was traditionally held by the nobility or the Crown. Therefore, the new world represented the only real opportunity to advance himself and any family he might be fortunate enough to begin.

He was joined in British North America by a flood of people fleeing the revolution in the United States. Among them was the family of his eventual wife, my great-great-great-great-grandmother, Elizabeth Quick. Her family had deep roots in the new world having been among the very first settlers in New Amsterdam, now called Manhattan. A map drawn in 1660 of New Amsterdam was annotated with all the home owners' names, including Teunis Quick who was Elizabeth's ancestor. His home was beside the fort which guarded the settlement, a fort which he, a mason, helped to build. The Quick family moved to New Jersey after the British bought New Amsterdam from the Dutch and from there moved to Upper Canada after the American Revolution. Clearly, the pioneering spirit ran deep in her family.

I have found many details surrounding the lives of William and Elizabeth but I have struggled to know them. Their lives reflect the early history of this country and there is something about them that defies easy description. To hack away at the wild forest to begin a life of self-sufficiency in a home of their own construction is something alien to our current ways and difficult to imagine. There were no roads, no electricity, no grocery stores, no hospitals and no cities upon which they could rely. Despite their quite different backgrounds, or perhaps because of them, they would have been proud and fierce defenders of their new home and the family that they raised.

But the most important thing I found was something to which my mind kept coming back over and over again. Learning that I was the descendant of an officer who fought and died in the War of 1812 was at first a curiosity, but something about how William arrived at that end caused me to want to know more about his life and times. It did not take long to discover that there was a high probability that he would have met and even fought along side Tecumseh.

It was one of those happenstance moments that strike when least expected. Oddly enough, the link between William and Tecumseh was echoed in my own youth when I attended Tecumseh Secondary School in Chatham. That the name Tecumseh was associated not only with my ancestor but also with my academic past was the unlikely spark that ignited my desire to write this book. It completely changed my opinion of Tecumseh and the War of 1812 from being a boring classroom experience to being a very real part of my own past. It allowed me to see that watershed epoch in Canadian history in a whole new light.

For months, I read as much as I could about the war as it was conducted in Southwestern Ontario. But that really only whetted my appetite to know William and Elizabeth better. I realized that I had to dig deeper into the historical records to do justice to their story. Doing so caused much frustration since each new finding seemed only to generate more questions.

As time passed, I found myself dreaming of the couple, both at night and during the day when my mind would wander. Then, almost imperceptibly, the misty fog of my dreams lifted and I finally saw them as real flesh and blood people. My imagination had given them life and I was able, at last, to start writing about their lives.

Today we scarcely give a thought to the difficulties the first settlers of this country endured, but as I have learned more about William and Elizabeth, I have been truly humbled. He carved two homes out of the wilderness with only the support of a handful of distant neighbours. During their twelve years of marriage, William and

Elizabeth raised six children, all of whom survived into adulthood. And when William perished in defence of their home, Elizabeth persevered, marrying Joshua Adams in 1820 and living to the remarkable age of seventy-three.

William's loyalty to the English crown may have been ambivalent because of his Scottish heritage but his duty to family and hopes for a future as master of his own estate would have been a powerful incentive to bury any such feelings. So after twelve years of happiness raising a family in peace and tranquillity, there is little doubt in my mind that William was highly motivated to defend his country against the invaders.

William was given the rank of Captain and made commander of the Marine Company in the First Essex Regiment. The function of a Marine Company in the regular British forces was two-fold. They were trained as infantry but served aboard the ships of the Royal Navy. Their primary task was to shoot the sailors manning an enemy vessel, thereby making its capture easier. Their other function was to guard the stores and rations. Considering that most sailors were recruited by press-gangs and could not always be trusted, this task was one of honour and importance.

Since naval warfare on the upper Great Lakes was somewhat limited until the Americans launched their new fleet in 1813 from Presque Isle (now Erie), Pennsylvania, the primary duty of the Marine Company would have been to keep the naval ships secure as they ferried troops around the western part of Lake Erie. Once the troops were safely landed, the company would have provided supporting fire for the flank companies of the regiment which, along with the regulars, would have formed the main assault forces. William commanded forty-two men in the company including a lieutenant and an ensign as his subordinate officers, four sergeants and thirty-six privates. He was paid the rather substantial salary of £12/1/6p a month, although it was held back three months to deter desertion.

Comparing William's wages to a private in his company, the private would have earned only 6/6 a month. In the old sterling, there were 20 shillings to a pound and 12 pence to a shilling. Converting William's wages to pence, he would have been earning 2,898 pence per month. His privates earned a meagre 78 pence a month which was just under three percent of their Captain's wages. The gap between officers and men was just another fact of life at the beginning of the eighteenth century.

As an officer at Fort Amherstburg, William would have dined with Major-General Sir Isaac Brock, Lieutenant-General Tecumseh (the Chief of the Shawnee tribe was given the rank out of deference to his position among the First Nations), Colonel (later Brigadier-General) Proctor and Captain William Caldwell of Caldwell's Rangers fame. While the differences in rank would have been a social barrier to any deep conversation, William would have been present as these great men planned the defence of the colonies. He would also have heard Tecumseh speak of his dreams for a great alliance of First Nations ruling their own land. Even Sir Isaac was said to have been quite taken by Tecumseh's wisdom and eloquence.

William led his men during the initial victories in 1812 and struggled with them through the difficult battles of 1813. The company took part in the Battle of Brownstone, the Battle of Maguaga, the capture of Detroit, the defeat of the American counter-offensive at Frenchtown (which the Americans refer to as the Battle of Raisen River), the First Siege of Fort Meigs, the Battle of the Miami and the Second Siege of Fort Meigs. With the exception of the two sieges at Fort Meigs, the British with their Shawnee and other First Nations allies, conducted a very strong defence marked by aggressively attacking the American supply lines and keeping the western flank of the Canadas safe from the aggressor.

However, the two sieges of Fort Meigs drained the British strength and made their native allies doubt the British resolve. The second siege of Fort Meigs took place in July, 1813, and was the last real offensive action by the British on the border between the Michigan Territory and the Western Region of Upper Canada.

Then, in August, 1813, the war on the western front took a dramatic turn for the worse when the American fleet won a decisive victory during the Battle of Lake Erie. When the smoke cleared, the Americans had either sank or captured the entire British fleet on the lake.

The fate of William and Elizabeth seemed destined to parallel the fortunes of the British forces. While the details are sketchy, the known time line of William's service record would suggest that he was probably wounded during the second siege of Fort Meigs. It is known that he did not take part in the Battle of Lake Erie, which supports the hypothesis that his wounds kept him under doctor's care at Fort Amherstburg throughout the late summer of 1813. According to one official document, William succumbed to "disease", but that may simply indicate that he died of an infection, a common cause of death for many soldiers. Sadly, many who survived their immediate wounds on the battlefield, died under doctor's care as there was little understanding of the importance of sterile conditions and there were no effective weapons against serious infection.

So William passed into history at Fort Amherstburg on September 19, 1813, just a few days before it was abandoned by the British on September 23. With the British supply lines completely undefended, General Proctor finally decided that he had no choice but to abandon Essex County to the Americans. He ordered the destruction of the fort to avoid it falling into enemy hands but, in their haste, the British not only demolished the fort but also lost the records of William's final resting place.

As the British began their retreat, the Americans crossed Lake Erie in hot pursuit, landing just south of Amherstburg on September 27. That date marked the beginning of their occupation of Essex County.

As the Americans chased the British up the Thames valley, Chief Tecumseh led two delaying actions against them in an effort to protect the British rear. The first was the Battle of The Forks (October 3) and the second was the Battle of Moraviantown (October 4). It was at Moraviantown where Tecumseh met his death.

Thus, in a little over two weeks, Elizabeth's world totally collapsed, starting with William's death and ending with the death of Tecumseh and the British retreat. She must have lived in a state of despair during the twenty-two months of American occupation.

The treaty ending the war was signed in December, 1814, but the Americans remained in Essex County until July 1, 1815. On that date, they relinquished Fort Malden, the new fort they had built on the foundations of Fort Amherstburg, and departed from Upper Canada.

232

Thomas Jefferson had characterized the war as a mere march through the remaining British colonies where crowds would welcome the Americans as liberators. While Jefferson's assessment was clearly in error, the Americans did come very close to "liberating" British North America through the use of brute force.

William was not a great general, like Sir Isaac Brock with whom he fought and to whom he would have been introduced and would have had at least professional relations, but he was a leader of men nevertheless who fought bravely to defend his family and home. Neither was he a leader of nations, like Chief Tecumseh, but he would have known the Chief from the period they both served at Fort Amherstburg. History pushed him into the company of great men and, like those great men, he shared their need to defend the important things in their lives.

I agonized for a long time how I should honour William and Elizabeth. I knew theirs was a good story but there were many gaps that made writing an accurate history impossible. Since I had never really attempted fictional writing, I remained in a quandary until I realized I could make William a writer, like myself, and have him create a "non-fictional account" of his adventures. It was a simple solution to my dilemma.

While I made William a writer, the only thing I have found actually written by William was his signature in a ledger acknowledging receipt of the pay for his men. It is a signature that is clear and elegant and I believe it reflects an honourable gentlemen, officer, husband and father. And those are the characteristics with which I endowed William in this book.

So while this "diary" is a work of fiction, it is a work based on the real lives of two human beings. In creating their world, I used the real names of their neighbours and relatives whenever I could find them. In fact, to the reader who wishes to do some research, there is only one name in this entire book that is purely fictional and not taken from the records of those who shared the life and times of William and Elizabeth.

I also made a great effort to ensure the accuracy of dates and events that would have been important to them both, even checking when Easter fell during those years.

Describing the topography, the flora, the rivers and their currents, the weather and even the clouds of mosquitoes ever present in Southwestern Ontario was relatively easy since I grew up in the area and know it well.

Finally, all Canadians will recognize the places and events of the War of 1812 that are described in the diary. Having read a number of first hand accounts from both sides, I tried to stay true to the facts as William might have seen them from his own perspective. Nevertheless, the historical record is incomplete so many details had to be invented to fill in the gaps. Hopefully my general knowledge of the period, places and events has allowed me to build plausible bridges across those voids.

It is unlikely that I shall ever know them better than I do today. But for me, the pride that grew as I discovered more and more about their lives is perhaps one of the most wonderful things I have ever experienced in my sixty years on this planet. Even though their story is only unique in its details, they survived and thrived like countless other early settlers and helped to build the foundation of this country.

Appendix 2:

The Facts About William and Elizabeth

I have no doubt that more information exists in some forgotten corner, eluding my eyes, but here, in chronological order, are the facts that I have been able to find about the lives of William and Elizabeth:

- **1774:** William was born in Kirkcudbright, Scotland. His father was John Buchanan (1747-1829) and his mother was Janet Thompson (1749-?). His parents were married on December 28, 1769, and William was their first child. Kirkcudbright is a small village at the mouth of the River Dee on the Irish Sea. Lord Selkirk, Earl of Kirkcudbright, was also born in this village and went on to fame in Canada for the Selkirk settlements in Manitoba. Kirkcudbright, like many Scottish towns, started to decline in population before the turn of the nineteenth century due to the introduction of large scale industrial farming. The Rev. Robert Muter wrote a report on the parish of Kirkcudbright for the King in 1792-1793 in which he detailed the land and economy. As a sea port, fishing and offshore trade were important as were the orchards and grain crops. However, the good reverend bemoans the decline in population, particularly in the 15-24 age group, and blames the lure of the new world. On a brighter note, he does describe the schools in Kirkcudbright as being of better than average quality and praises the village's handling of the poor. It is likely therefore that William received enough formal education that he could read and write proficiently.

- **1782:** I have found two different birth places cited for Elizabeth, one in Amwell, New Jersey, the other in Colchester Township, Essex County, Ontario, Canada. The only evidence to support which birthplace is correct is the chronology of other events. Her parents and grandparents fled to Canada as Loyalists which probably would have been around the time of the Treaty of Paris in 1783, a year after her birth. That would, therefore, be at least circumstantial evidence to confirm her place of birth as New Jersey rather than Canada. Her father was John Alexander Quick (1750-1820) and her mother was Elizabeth Stout (1734-1807). One source cited her mother's death as occurring in 1828, but there is no solid evidence for this. As stated above, her grandfather, Cornelius Quick (1729-1790), brought the entire family from New Jersey to Canada following the American Revolution and was given land in Essex County as a Loyalist. Elizabeth had a rich family history, particularly her own great-great-great-great-grandfather, the Dutch immigrant Theunis Quick (1600-1666), who helped establish the colony of New Amsterdam (now Manhattan) and was among the first 200 settlers there. A famous map of New Amsterdam drawn in 1660 shows the home of Theunis, who was a mason by trade, directly across the street from the fort he helped build. Today, that address would place it near the new "One World Trade Center" tower in lower Manhattan.

- **1784/08/21:** The only record of a "William Buchanan" immigrating to North America before 1800 cites the arrival of a William Buchanan in Nova Scotia in 1784. The record indicates that he was alone with no dependants.

- **1787:** An informal census of Nova Scotia was taken over the course of a couple of years from 1786 to 1789 and lists a "William Buchanan" as the sole resident and "head of household" at a Queen's County location. From this point until William marries Elizabeth, the trail of his life goes cold. Yet, he must have left Nova Scotia sometime during the mid-1790's in order to have had enough time to carve another new home out of the wilderness and then to meet Elizabeth and court her. It is inconceivable that he could have done all that in a single year or even two.

- **1800:** William and Elizabeth were married.

- **1802/02:** The couple was blessed with their first child, a son, and named him John D. I have not discovered for what the "D" stands. The actual date of the birth is also not known. John died in 1843.

236

- **1804:** I was surprised to learn that two of William's brothers, John and Gordon, signed up with Lord Selkirk to sail to the Baldoon settlement which was not very far from where William had settled in Essex County. Mention is made in a number of sources about Robert Buchanan, one of John's sons and therefore William's nephew, passing away during the voyage. Robert was ten years old.

- **1805:** William's second child was born, another son. They named him Andrew. Andrew died on March 8, 1888.

- **1807/01/25:** William's third child, another son, was born. Named after his father, William Jr. died on August 26, 1875. He followed in his father's footsteps, also reaching the rank of Captain in the militia. William Jr. is my great-great-great-grandfather.

- **1808/03/02:** William and Elizabeth finally celebrated the birth of the first daughter, Helen, who passed away on July 19, 1884.

- **1810:** Elizabeth gave birth to another daughter, Hannah, who passed away on October 23, 1846.

- **1811:** Elizabeth had William's sixth and last child. It was another daughter, thereby reaching equilibrium in the home with three girls and three boys. Their last daughter, Eliza Jane, survived to the remarkable age of 91, passing away in 1902.

- **1812/07/12:** Documents show that William arrived at Fort Amherstburg on this date with his company. He was docked pay for the number of days in July that passed before his arrival. The record indicated that he was "absent with cause". I could not find any documentation concerning how William achieved his rank of Captain. Normally, militia ranks were awarded based on the number of "friends" a man could bring along with him. Perhaps William was a very persuasive man among his peers in the eastern part of the county. There is equally no evidence of why they were formed into a Marine Company. A "marine company" in the Royal Navy was more respected than the press-ganged sailors that manned His Majesty's warships. The marines were often used to guard the ship's stores and as marksmen to pick off enemy sailors in the rigging of their ships. Perhaps William's Scottish background growing up by the sea and his more recent voyage across the ocean were factors in this decision. In any case, my research led me to the web site of the National Archives where I found a microfilmed copy of the original hand-written ledgers documenting the pay he and his company received in October for their service in July. And when I scrolled through the document, I was truly dumbfounded when I saw his actual signature acknowledging that he had received the money that was owed to his company. While the linkage between Tecumseh and William was the initial trigger for this work, it was that heart-stopping moment when I saw his own handwriting on my computer screen late one night that galvanized my resolve to finish the book. That single image captured from a two hundred year old hand-written piece of paper continues to inspire me each and every time I look at it. Here it is:

- **1813:** I have found third party documentation stating that William was present at the Battles of Frenchtown and Fort Meigs. But I found it hard to imagine that he and his company did not have a role to play in the capture of Detroit. Then the National Archives came to the rescue again and I found the microfilmed copy of a report written by Major Reynolds, a British regular, listing the officers who took part in the capture of Detroit. Sure enough, William's name was on the list, proving his participation in the "Reduction of Detroit", as the Major named it.

- **1813/09/19:** There is conflicting information concerning the cause of William's death, but all sources agree on the date. It was just a few days before General Proctor ordered the destruction of Fort Amherstburg to avoid it being used by the enemy. But in carrying out his orders, the location of William's final resting place was lost. That makes me rather more sad than how he actually died. It is very probable that he died as a result of an infection which would explain one "official" source listing the cause of his death as "disease". If he were seriously wounded at the Second Battle of Fort Meigs, an infection may have developed while he was in hospital. At that time, it was common for many soldiers to die as a result of the poor care they received post-battlefield. Doctors simply did not know how to treat or prevent many common types of infections which, as a result, were often fatal.

*   *   *

After the war, Elizabeth got married again in 1820 to Joshua Adams (1784-1856). She had been granted a pension related to William's war-time service, but the amount is unknown and was not likely a huge amount. In any case, raising six children and managing the homestead by herself would have been very difficult, so re-marrying was a logical course of action. Elizabeth had five more children with Joshua:

Mary Ann (November 4, 1821 to March 28, 1871)
Matthew (April 13, 1823 to ?)
Uretta (1825 to April 9, 1895)
Joshua (April 15, 1826 to ?)
Ann Louisa (June 1, 1828 to ?)

As a result of her two marriages, Elizabeth raised eleven children and despite that enormous effort, or perhaps because of the strength it demonstrated, she lived to the ripe old age of seventy-three, well beyond the average for women in those days. She passed away on September 27, 1855, and is buried in a cemetery near Leamington.

Appendix 3:

The First Pay List for the Marine Company

I found this record, dated October 27, 1812, while browsing through the National Archives web site. It had been microfilmed from the original payroll records of the Company thereby making it accessible to anyone with the patience to search through thousands of images. It was the document upon which William had placed his signature attesting that he had received the money owing to his men. I attempted to accurately transcribe the names of his men as they were listed but there are some names (indicated by a "?") that are likely misspelled because I could not interpret, with confidence, the author's handwriting.

All of the company reported for duty at Fort Amherstburg on July 12 and were thus only paid for part of a month's service. They were the last company to report, possibly because they had the furthest to travel, coming all the way from Colchester Township which is at the far south-eastern corner of the county.

While the Militia Acts of 1793 and 1794 in Upper Canada made participation in the militia mandatory for all males age 16 to 60, many men simply did not register. In 1808, Upper Canada consolidated all its legislation regarding the militia, and made twice-yearly training a minimum standard. When war broke out, though, many men abandoned their units and desertion from the militia was a wide-spread problem. When William's company was ordered north as part of the effort to defend against the initial American invasion across the Detroit River in July of 1812, most of his men simply disappeared into the wilderness. It was gratifying to see, though, that most of those who vanished did return to duty within a few weeks. Later in the war, deserters were punished by being branded.

To ease the problem of desertion, it was common practice to allow the men to go home for a limited time to tend their farms. Without this flexibility, their families might very well have starved over the winter.

There were also allowances given to soldiers and their families consisting of various food stuffs, animal feed and cloth for clothing. It should be remembered that these goods were possibly of greater importance to frontier survival than the small remuneration the ordinary soldiers received. See Appendix 4 for a list of the goods received in addition to their pay. It should be noted, however, that men serving in the militia were given these extras only at the discretion of the local commander of the regular forces. I could not discover if William's men received these extras or not.

When examining the list of who served in William's company, there are a few names that stand out. For example, Private Cornelius Quick was likely Elizabeth's cousin. Private William Munger was likely the brother of Elizabeth's sister-in-law, Susanna Quick (née Munger), making him a distant brother-in-law. One might wonder if having close relatives under his command was a problem for William. In fact, there appears to have been quite a number of men who were related to at least one other man in the company, as evidenced by the number of names ending in "Brush", "Heighly", "Wilkison", "Fox", "Brunner" and "Whittle". Of note, there were two individuals named "John Whittle" plus one other "Whittle". It is very likely that this was a father and his two sons. Remarkably, even this early in our history, it is possible to see the diversity within William's company which included men of English, French, Dutch and German descent. It should not surprise that Canada's multicultural heritage has deep roots.

From the numbers, it would appear that virtually every male who could fire a musket in Colchester Township enlisted in the militia. Not only was that a success for the colonial administration but, more importantly, it showed that the community was strongly committed to the protection of their homes and families.

Here is the roll of William's company in July of 1812:

Officers:

Captain William Buchanan
("Absent with Cause" - July 1 to July 11)[1]
Lieutenant John Brush
("Absent with Cause" - July 1 to July 11)[2]

Ensign James Stockwell
(deserted on July 19)[3]

Sergeants:

John Fullmer (deserted July 19, returned August 8)
Joseph Heighly (deserted July 16, returned August 9)
Robert McMurry (deserted July 19)
John Barthdette (deserted July 19)

Privates:

John Brown
John Hitchcock (deserted July 13, returned August 9)
William Munger (deserted July 13)[4]
John Elliott (deserted July 13, returned August 20)
Thomas Williams (deserted July 13)
Frances Wilkison (deserted July 13)
Alexander Wilkison (deserted July 13, returned August 8)
Nicholas LaBallaine (deserted July 14)
Thomas Green (deserted July 14)
Silvester Sommers (deserted July 14)
Henry Starks (deserted July 14)
Mickel Fox (deserted July 14, returned August 9)
George Fox (deserted July 14, returned August 12)
Christopher Heighly (deserted July 14, returned August 9)
Jacob de la Camp (deserted July 14)
John Fox (deserted July 14, returned August 12)
Nathan Baldwin (deserted July 15, returned August 12)
John Hewit (deserted July 15, returned August 7)
Abel Augustin (deserted July 15)
Adam Bruner (deserted July 15, returned August 8)
Henry Bruner (deserted July 15, returned August 9)
Ezekiel Boring (deserted July 15, returned August 9)
Jacob Alleh (?) (deserted July 15)
Jacob Fox (deserted July 15, returned August 9)
Cornelius Quick (deserted July 16, returned August 8)[5]
Chester Beeman (deserted July 16, returned August 9)
Thomas Bell (deserted July 18, returned August 8)
Rudolph Hoffman (deserted July 18, returned August 8)
James Gamble (deserted July 19, returned August 8)

242

William Roberts (deserted July 18, returned August 7)
Joseph Bezeau (deserted July 19, returned August 9)
Silas Brush (deserted July 19, returned August 8)
John Brush (deserted July 19, returned August 8)
John Sipes (?) (deserted July 19, returned August 7)
Lewis Lavoit (deserted July 19, returned August 7)
William Harsffy (deserted July 19, returned August 8)
Richmond Roads (deserted July 19, returned August 10)
John Whittle (deserted July 19, returned August 9)
John Heighly (deserted July 19, returned August 7)
Theodore Malotte (deserted July 19, returned August 8)
James Piggot (deserted July 19)
Abel Whittle (deserted July 19)
Davis Lloyd (deserted July 19, returned August 8)
John Whittle (deserted July 19)
Adam Lleery (deserted July 19, returned August 9)
Samuel McKee (deserted July 19, returned August 9)

Notes:

[1] As a result of being absent for a good part of July, William was docked almost half a month's pay, receiving £6-11-6d instead of £12-1-6d for July.

[2] Just as William was penalized, Lieutenant Brush was docked almost half a month's pay, receiving £4-4-6d, instead of £7-9-6d for July.

[3] Since Ensign Stockwell had not yet reported back, he forfeited his entire pay for the month of July (£4-4-0d).

[4] William Munger was likely the brother of Susanna Munger who married Elizabeth's eldest brother, Joseph, in 1810 and was, therefore, a distant brother-in-law to William.

[5] Cornelius Quick was likely a nephew of Elizabeth's father and thus her cousin.

Appendix 4:

Military Supplies and Equipment

According to the book "Officers of the British Forces in Canada During the War of 1812-15" written by L. Homfray Irving for the Canadian Military Institute and published by the Welland Tribune Print in 1908, the following food stuffs and other goods were supplied by the crown to the soldiers and their families during the war.

RATIONS

The Daily Allotment from September 1811 to April 1812:

> Flour - 1.0 lbs.
> Pork - 1.43 lbs.
> Fresh Beef - 1.0 lbs.
> Peas - 0.43 pints
> Rice - 1.15 oz.

The Daily Allotment from April 1812 to August, 1813:
(The major difference from the earlier allotment was that pork was removed and butter added.)

> Flour - 1.0 lbs.
> Fresh Beef - 1.0 lbs.
> Peas - 0.43 pints
> Rice - 1.15 oz.
> Butter - 0.85 oz.

The Monthly Allotment after August 1813:
(As the war progressed, the frequency of allotments was reduced as well as the amounts. But if either fresh or salt beef was available, the men could take that instead of the salt pork. If they took the beef option, it was limited to 1 lb. rather than the larger amount available if they stayed with the pork. A "gill" [pronounced like the girl's name Jill] was equal to one-quarter of a pint and was only issued when the men were in camp. They could not take it home.)

Flour or Biscuits - 1.5 lbs.
Salt Pork - 10.5 oz.
Rum - 0.5 gill

ANIMAL FORAGE
(No allotments were given to the militia for their horses or draught animals since it was presumed they could feed their own animals from their own farms.)

The Weekly Allotment for Horses

Hay - 1 bundle (16 lbs.)
Straw - 2 bundles (24 lbs.)

The Weekly Allotment for Draught Horses or Oxen

Oats - 8 qts. (8.5 lbs.)
Hay - 1.75 bundles (20 lbs.)
Straw - 2 bundles (24 lbs.)

ARMS

According to the Militia Act of Upper Canada, each man was required to supply the following at his own expense:

1 musket
1 bayonet
1 cartouche box (a cartouche carried the charge for the musket)
1 bayonet strap and scabbard
1 musket sling
1 breastplate

UNIFORMS
(Each man had to provide his own uniform. Militia officers had uniforms that were similar to the regular British army. However, the rank and file uniforms were very distinctive. Their uniforms are described below.)

Effective January 1813:

Green jackets; red cuffs and collar; white lace; blue gun-mouth trousers; felt regulation cap.

Effective July 1813:

Green jackets; yellow facings

PRIZE MONEY

Prize Money was also awarded for certain victories, such as the capture of Detroit, based on the value of the armaments and supplies captured. As it happened, the only prize money awarded on the Essex/Michigan frontier was for that capture. It was split according to a complex formula of "shares", the Commander receiving 100 shares while privates received one share each. Each share was worth £3.

Tecumseh as leader of the "Indians" received eight shares, the same as the highest non-commissioned officers. Did the British really respect the rank they gave him of Lieutenant-General or was it all window dressing?

As a captain, William would have received 16 shares, or £48, an enormous sum and substantially more than the commander of the entire aboriginal allied force.

www.ingramcontent.com/pod-product-compliance
Lightning Source LLC
LaVergne TN
LVHW051502080426
835509LV00017B/1876